coping
with
CASH

PETER COREY
illustrated by
Mike Phillips

Scholastic Children's Books
Commonwealth House, 1-19 New Oxford Street
London WC1A 1NU, UK

A division of Scholastic Ltd
London ~ New York ~ Toronto ~ Sydney ~ Auckland
Mexico City ~ New Delhi ~ Hong Kong

First published in the UK by Scholastic Ltd, 2000

Text copyright © Peter Corey, 2000
Illustrations copyright © Mike Phillips, 2000

ISBN 0 439 01015 2

Typeset by TW Typesetting, Midsomer Norton, Somerset
Printed by Cox & Wyman Ltd, Reading, Berks.

10 9 8 7 6 5 4 3 2 1

The right of Peter Corey and Mike Phillips to be identified as the author
and illustrator of this work respectively has been asserted by them in
accordance with the Copyright, Designs and Patents Act, 1988.

Contents

Dedication

This book is dedicated to Peter Martin, the best accountant an author could possibly have. Without him I wouldn't have any cash to write about!

DO YOU NEED THIS BOOK ?

Hello! It's your favourite author here! Oh. Sorry. That's a bit of a presumption really, isn't it? After all, you may never have read anything by me.

Who am I, anyway? Check the front cover. I'll wait.

Dum, dum, dee-dum dee-dum.

You back? Good.

No. I'm not Mike Phillips. Try again.

Dee dee-diddly dee dee dee.

I'd whistle but I don't know how to write it.

Back again? Right. Do you know who I am now?

No! I'm not Hippo! I'm Peter Corey. Got it? Good.

And what I want to know is…

Do you need this book?

Well, if you've never read any of my books you probably need to know that if you don't like laughing then this book is not for you.[1]

Also, if you're not interested in finding out loads of useful[2] stuff then this book is probably not for you either.

Likewise if you've got no cash then this book is definitely not for you, because you can't afford it.[3] But

---

1: If you HAVE read any of my books you probably need to know that as well!
2: OK – useless.
3: Unless you're borrowing it from a library, in which case it's free as long as you take it back on time.

that's what this book is about – CASH. Getting it, losing it, holding on to it, spending it; even sniffing it and building totally pointless *Blue Peter*-style hamster cages out of it, probably. Because this book covers everything you can possibly do with money, and a few things that you can't. It tells you how money started, and some truly amazing facts about it – such as...

HANG ON! You haven't paid for it yet! So I'll leave you to sort that out and look forward to meeting you again at the start of chapter one (over the page). If you don't sort it out (i.e. don't get to own the book because you can't afford to buy it) then all I can say is that it's been nice meeting you anyway. By the way – what did you say your name was? Peter Corey? Oh no – that's me! Doh!

WHAT IS MONEY?

Welcome, new book owner. You're now a few pounds worse off. However you are about to discover all there is to know about cash. How to spend it and how to hang on to it.[1] Incidentally, if you haven't bought this book but are still reading it, then just make sure that you don't dribble or sneeze on it – somebody else might want to buy it you know.

Anyway, if you now own this book you probably dipped your hand in your pocket and pulled out a bit of money. Or you may have whinged on and on and on until your parent dipped their hand in their pocket and pulled out a bulging wallet. Or an old sock with a few coins tied in the corner, because people keep their money in all sorts of strange places: under floorboards, under mattresses, on top of wardrobes – even in *banks*! Weird!

1: Don't buy silly books for a start! Only joking!

You see, money makes people behave in very strange ways and do very peculiar things. But what exactly *is it*?

Turning to the *Oxford Pocket Dictionary*, which as you all know by now is so big that it's almost as large as Prince Edward's bald patch, we find out the following:

money : (Munny)
Pieces of gold, silver, copper etc., stamped with government authority to be used as a medium of exchange.

moneybags : (Munibagz)

Which presumably means to buy stuff. I love the way they say "gold, silver and copper etc." It just shows you how old my copy of the *Pocket Oxford* is. These days money is made out of anything that can be recycled without it falling apart. Anything other than gold, silver, copper etc., anyway.

The *Big Book of Contemporary Slang* tells us that money can also be called Dosh, Wongar, Cash, Gelt, Folding Stuff, Loose Change, Readies and any number of other things. None of which helps you get it.

Shakespeare tells us that "a fool and his money are soon parted." Not only a fool, actually; a quite sensible person, with no intention of spending anything, and *their* money are soon parted, especially if the person doing the parting is a time-share salesperson, or someone carrying a very large gun.[1]

The Bible on the other hand tells us that: "Money answereth all things"; all things, that is, except you when you're looking for it. You know the score – you're

1: Or both.

late for the school bus, your only fifty pee has gone walk-about and you're standing in the middle of the lounge going: "Fifty pee! Where are you? Come to me now, PPPLLEEEAAASSSEEEE!!!" And does it? Does it diddly! It hides, keeping as quiet as only a fifty pee can, until you positively have to run for the bus. And what happens when you come home? That very same fifty pence piece is sitting on the sofa, bold as brass,[1] almost smiling at you, as if to say: "I've been here all the time. In fact, I've spent the morning watching Richard and Judy. They're worth their weight in gold."

"Worth their weight in gold": just one of the many expressions that some people say which relate to money – well, gold anyway. It basically means that somebody is very good at something and well worth having around. So in Richard and Judy's[2] case it would be the wrong expression to use. "Neither use nor ornament" might be a better one! But in fact there are lots of expressions and sayings relating to money, such as...

"Money talks": although we've just found out that it doesn't.

1: Well – bold as reconstituted elephant droppings, which is probably what they make money out of these days.
2: For anyone from the planet Fibron, or somewhere other than the UK, Richard and Judy are TV personalities, apparently.

"Money has no smell": which means that however money is obtained there's no stigma attached to the actual money itself. People also refer to "dirty money" meaning money obtained in a dishonest or dishonourable way, which doesn't include money got by cleaning your dad's car, although it probably should! The expression "Money has no smell" was first used by Vespasian, who was Emperor of Rome from AD 69–79. Apart from building the Coliseum and introducing a more comprehensive education system (so it's *his* fault!), Vespasian also introduced a tax on public lavatories.

When his son Titus complained that the tax was unfair, Vespasian held up a coin that had been collected via the loo tax and said: "Does it smell?" Titus admitted that it didn't. "That's funny," said Vespasian, "It should do – I've just fished it out of the lavatory bowl!"

"Money is the root of all evil": meaning that everything bad is caused by money. Certainly money causes trouble, but I can't believe that *every* bad thing is caused by money. I'll take my chances, anyway!

"Money makes money": meaning that if you've got money you've got more chance of making more. Well, in my experience if you've got money you've got more chance of spending it!

"Money doesn't grow on trees": meaning that money isn't just lying around the place, except of course at the Royal Mint. In fact some money *does* grow on trees, in that some money is made of paper and paper comes from wood pulp, which comes from trees. But that doesn't make it any easier to get hold of.

I THOUGHT I'D CUT OUT THE MIDDLE MAN!

The fact that people make up sayings and proverbs about money shows how important it has always been. But it doesn't stop at proverbs. Have you ever heard anyone, maybe your granny, mention pin money? She's probably mentioned it in between telling you how important string is. No? Doesn't ring any bells? I'm not surprised. After all, it's not always easy to work out what she's on about. But if you have heard her talk about pin money you might even have wondered what it meant. Well, it isn't just the ramblings of someone who would be better off living on another planet (even though she probably would), it actually means something. These days it usually refers to a small amount of money not really worth thinking about, such as bad wages (as in "I've just got a Saturday job at the local branch of Burger Barons – I'm working for pin money"). But in the days when many women looked after the house and only men went out to work, it referred to money that a

11

husband gave his wife for her to spend on herself (again not usually very much). So what exactly *is* pin money? Simple – money for pins! Pins were invented in France in 1543, and Catherine Howard[1] was the first person in England to use them.

They were considered a real luxury and not suitable for common people. Therefore, they were only on sale for two days of each year, some time in January. Husbands would give their wives money to buy these pins at the start of the year. Fascinating! Any husband who tried that now would get his head bitten off, particularly as many women have careers of their own and therefore their own money; which means that they can buy whatever they like – including pins.

1: Fifth wife of Henry VIII.

Ah – money! We couldn't survive without it. Or could we? How do people who literally have no money survive? How did people manage before money was invented?

Let's start with that question and work our way through to the trickier ones. Yes! It's time to strap on a large drinking flask, slip into our jelly shoes and go trekking through the golden sands of time, trying to avoid poisonous sand snakes and ignoring the mirages. Ready? Let's go!

How money first started

It's not much fun living in a village that is largely made of mud. At least, that's what Wart Fatface thought, as he rubbed a damp clod of earth around his face. Wart had only recently moved to Floodybridge, a small village consisting mostly of a few houses, a church and … er … a bridge that was regularly flooded. They really knew how to name things in those days.

Wart got his name from the large wart on the end of his nose. His surname came from the fact that he had a very fat face. His name was originally Wartnose V. Fatface,[1] but he had it changed by deedpoll. Things could have been  worse. He could have been the bloke up the road with the terrible acne and hideous wind problem.[2]

Wart knew only too well that once you'd settled in a new village, the trick was to start a trade. After all, that  was the only way to survive. Take Bigears Baker, for instance. He made the bread. Then there was Beerbelly Cooper who made the barrels for Nothumbs Brewer, who made the beer. He got his name from the  fact that he had no thumbs; he lost them in an unfortunate exploding Christmas punch incident. There was also Gorgeous Stitcher, who made exotic clothes for  Snooty Bighouse, who owned the castle on the hill. In fact, everybody had a worthwhile occupation.

Everybody except Wart that was. The problem was that you had to have something to trade. Money didn't exist. If Beerbelly Cooper wanted a loaf, he'd offer Bigears Baker a barrel for it. A small barrel, obviously. But what happened if Beerbelly didn't have a small barrel, only large ones? Well, they probably worked out

1: The "V" stood for Very.
2: I'll let you work his name out for yourself!

a system whereby a barrel would be worth – say – 20 loaves, and Beerbelly would have to trust Bigears to make a note of how many loaves he owed him; which was a problem, because Bigears couldn't write. Even if he could, it wouldn't have helped, because Beerbelly couldn't read. Reading and writing were for posh folk like Snooty Bighouse. Oh yes – you could really go places if you could read. Except the library, obviously, because libraries didn't exist then.

But how was somebody like Wart, with nothing to trade, going to survive in this sort of environment? Well, he could do little jobs for people, and receive goods in exchange. For instance, he could help Beerbelly make barrels, for which Beerbelly might give him a bit of wood. Wart could then trade this bit of wood with Bigears Baker for a loaf.

But there was a problem with this system: suppose Bigears didn't want a bit of wood? Wart would have to trade his wood with somebody else (who did want wood), in order to get something that Bigears wanted, so that Wart could get his loaf. This was called bartering, but as you can see it was pretty complicated. Something needed to be found that could replace the various goods that people wanted to trade, so that people could get the stuff they needed quickly and without a huge fuss – or before they starved to death!

The stone money age

In England, in around 3,500 BC they started using flint to barter, because flint was really useful for making arrow heads, axes and little flint novelties for the tourist trade.

I suppose the only problem with that was how much flint you had to "pay" to get what you wanted. Was your bit of flint big enough to buy a loaf or only a couple of sandwiches?

A few odd coppers

In Egypt, in about 2,500 BC (which is over four millennia ago), they started using copper rings as "money". Again I suppose the value of the ring depended on its size and thickness, and this probably led to lots of arguments.

Copper was obviously something that they had lots of, just as England had plenty of flint. At about the same

16

time in Mesopotamia, they found that they had plenty of silver, and barley, lying around, and so they started using that as "money". And because they weighed the silver they knew exactly how much it was worth. They made it into small lumps called shekels, which all weighed the same. This was a much better system, because it was easier to tell how much the silver was worth. I expect they weighed the barley as well.

If you're wondering where Mesopotamia is, I'll tell you: it's in Iraq. In fact it *is* Iraq. They changed the name from Mesopotamia to Iraq, probably because nobody could spell Mesopotamia. Mind you, I sometimes have a bit of trouble spelling Irak – sorry, I mean Iraq.

That'll do ricely!

Shekels didn't catch on everywhere. The ancient Chinese used rice for money. That must have been a bit tricky. Imagine running around with your pockets full of rice. One quick game of touch rugby and you've lost half of it. Also, there's the problem of swelling. Anyone knows that if you get rice wet it swells. So imagine you're out on the town, pockets full of rice, determined to have a great time. Suddenly it starts to rain, your rice swells and you can't get it out of your pocket. Not a lot of use if you're trying to impress your date!

I'VE HEARD OF INFLATION, BUT THIS IS RIDICULOUS!

Realizing that rice money had it's own problems, the Chinese introduced money in the shape of miniature gardening tools. I'm not quite sure what the exchange rate was, but maybe one spade was worth three hoes or something like that. Miniature gardening tools? I would have thought that those would be tricky to get out of your pocket as well!

Funny money

But gardening tools weren't the strangest things ever used for money. In Ghana they used pebbles made of quartz – this was before they started making watches out of it. The people of India used shells, Tibetans used metal discs, the Yap islanders used limestone discs and in Santa Cruz they used feathers. I don't fancy that! You'd stick your hand in your wallet and tickle yourself to death!

There has also been cocoa-bean money in Mexico, banana seeds in Uganda, lengths of telephone wire (!) in Tanzania, blocks of wood in Angola and eggs in Vietnam. Oh – and the people of Papua New Guinea used dogs' teeth. I wouldn't have fancied being a dog around there, would you?

As late as the fourteenth century (700 years ago) people in the Sahara desert were using salt as money. They kept it in large blocks and cut a bit off, the size of which depended on how much the goods they were buying were worth.

Raiding and trading

As civilizations grew, so they started exploring the areas around them. They quickly discovered that there were other people living near by. Explorers would return home and say: "There's this bunch of really strange people living over there. They look funny and talk funny, but they've got some very nice stuff that we haven't got, and it just might be worth having." In those days there were basically two ways to get your hands on somebody else's stuff; you could either take it by force, or trade it for something of your own. Sometimes it simply wasn't possible to take things by force; the other civilization was bigger and tougher than you were. The only option was to trade. Merchants from one country would load their ships with local goods and take them off to trade with other nations. For example, the Romans took oil, wine and wool and traded it for spices, grain and silk.

All this was fine and dandy if the things you had to trade with were small enough to get on a ship. But what if all you had to trade with was cattle? You couldn't get many cows on the average ship in those days, a lot of them died on the journey and you also couldn't be sure that the people at the other end would want them anyway. A better system needed to be created. Unfortunately that wasn't going to happen for a very, very long time.

Loose change

The first coins (as far as we know) were made in Lydia – or Western Turkey to you and me. They were made from mixing gold and silver to create a substance called electrum, then casting it into a rough pebble shape and stamping a picture on it; a lion in fact (not a turkey!). King Croesus (560–546 BC) had coins made of pure gold, which he had lots of.[1]

The Lydian coins were made in about 700 BC, and pretty soon other countries were copying the idea and inventing their own coins, most of them made of gold or silver. But why use such precious metals? Why not use a bit of old iron or something. The reason they used gold is because it looks nice, doesn't go rusty and it's also easy to hammer into shape and stamp a picture on. It's also quite rare, and so people couldn't start making their own coins and passing them off as the real thing – although I shouldn't think that that stopped them trying!

1: Hence the expression "as rich as Croesus".

"Heads"

The first ruler to have his head on a coin was Alexander the Great – the ruler of Lydia. When Julius Caesar was murdered the Romans brought out a special coin – a bit like the special commemorative coins we have these days. But coins were still only being used locally. They weren't being used to trade with other countries, who had their own coins.

Roman around with a pocket of dosh

As the Roman Empire expanded – that is to say, as the Roman army swept across Europe building roads, putting in plumbing and sticking their swords into any of the locals who complained – so the use of coins spread. The Romans had been using *rude* bronze, which didn't mean bits of bronze hammered into the shape of something naughty, but lumps of unworked bronze. Oh and they also used salt. Roman soldiers were paid in salt.[1] You can easily imagine the problem this gave them. For a start there really was nowhere in the soldier's uniform to store the salt; no pockets or anything.

I HAVE TO CARRY MY SALT AROUND IN MY HAND ALL DAY!

OH, NO. YOU WANT TO GET YOURSELF A NICE LITTLE CRUET SET, LIKE ME

1: This is where the expression "not worth his salt" comes from.

At night they could put it into the belly button on the front of their breastplate which obviously made it easy to stop people stealing it, but it was not ideal when you were on the march. The Roman authorities, who were on the ball, replaced salt and bronze with coins towards the end of the first century AD, mainly in order to pay their huge army, who were frankly getting fed up with being paid in salt, twigs, banana pips or anything else that happened to be currently serving as "money".

Of course, the soldiers couldn't actually spend the coins even when they got them. Imagine the scene: it's a lovely summer's Thursday evening in Gaulus (later to be known as France). Timurus and his pal Libatius have got the evening off. They've had a tough day putting peasants to the sword, and all they want now is to find a bar, have a few drinks and then maybe go on later to a disco.

They're stood at the bar of Le Olliday Inne, a popular night spot in those days. They're watching the cabaret, which seems to be some sort of local folk dancing. In fact, it's a couple of Gothic slaves leaping around barefoot on a large sheet of metal. There's a fire beneath the metal keeping it nice and warm, just in case they forget the dance steps.

The barman brings them a couple of glasses of the local wine – a wine so recently trod that it's still got bits of verruca floating in it. He is about to tell them how much it is when they slap a handful of small round bits of metal on the counter and tell him to *keep the change*. This is an instruction that he doesn't understand for a number of reasons:

1. He's French and speaks absolutely no Latin – having never felt the need to learn, and having never been to school.
2. He doesn't even know what *money* is, let alone *change*.

So that's two reasons, in fact. Anyway...

This conversation could have continued for a very long time, had not the Roman Empire collapsed and the soldiers gone back to Rome. But this was one of the big snags with money – it was all very well if you wanted to spend it in your own country, but if you were off on a conquering tour or having a bit of a foreign away break, you were completely stuck. Although it has to be remembered that the coins were often made from gold and silver, which are valuable in their own right. But there wasn't that much of it, so coins were quite rare.

And you couldn't spend them abroad, which is why things like salt and grain continued to be used for trading.

Salting it all away

Of course, things like salt weren't used to show how wealthy a person was. You didn't, for instance, hear people say things like: "That Abu Ben Nevis is a wealthy bloke – you should see the great piles of salt he's got!"

Wealth was measured in things like precious metal (gold and silver) made into jewellery; and cattle. People would say: "That Abu Ben Nevis is a wealthy bloke – he's got a hundred cows." Or maybe camels if you were living in the Sahara desert. Cows had also become an early form of currency. In fact the word pecuniary, which means *to do with money* comes from *pecus*, which is a Latin term for cattle.

Middle Age spread

By about the fifth century AD, after the fall of Rome, many European states were created and they each had their own coins, which were very nice looking but still no good if you wanted to travel. Sometimes individual cities would mint their own coins, and because the church was very powerful in those days, even bishops would issue their own coins. It all got very confusing, until money changers came into existence. These were like an early form of bank. You could take your coins issued by Derek the Bishop of Chester, and exchange them for the much nicer ones issued by Arthur the Briton, or if you were really lucky you might get your hands on some of those really unusual ones issued by Uthuck the Totally Stupid.

DEREK   ARTHUR   UTHUCK

You probably still wouldn't be able to spend them in your local Sainsbury's[1] though, because Sainsbury's were still hooked into the old barter system – this week's special offer was a chicken ("Keep it as a pet – then have it as a lunch!") which cost just three bits of flint and a feather.

1: This wasn't Sainsbury's as we know it, of course. It was a store run by Erthric Sainsbury, the Body Snatcher, whose meat counter was always particularly busy during periods of plague.

One world – one coin

It was totally impossible to set up one type of coin for the whole of the then-known world, for a lot of very good reasons. The main one is that the various countries of the world were far too busy fighting each other; so the idea that they might sit down and work out a currency that suited everybody was a total pipe dream. Let's face it, we can't even agree on one *now*,[1] so what chance did they have hundreds of years ago? In fact, in those days they couldn't even agree on one set of coins per country! This was mainly due to the fact that countries were divided into separate kingdoms with their own rulers. And each ruler wanted his or her head on a coin. And why not?

WHAT MAKES YOU THINK YOUR HEAD IS MORE SUITED TO A COIN THAN MINE?

It wasn't until 1066 and the Norman conquest that England became one powerful kingdom under William the first. But did this mean one set of coins for the whole country? Of course it didn't! But then ordinary people really didn't need money. They grew their own food and swapped (or bartered) any surplus for anything else they needed. But what William I did do was set a value for sterling silver, which meant that there was an agreed value for a particular size of lump of silver. Again this

---

1: At the time of writing, the UK is still trying to decide whether or not it wants the Euro.

didn't really affect the ordinary man in the street, because he didn't have any! Money was still very much a symbol of wealth and influence, neither of which your average Saxon peasant had.

The great leap forward

This system continued pretty well unchanged for several centuries. In fact, it remains unchanged in many parts of the world, where they've still not seen any great need to use cash. Very wise is all I can say! But what of the so-called "civilized" world? Well, we have to make a huge jump forward in time to see any really big change in the way things were done. So, all together now…

Worth the paper it's written on, probably

It wasn't until as late as the sixteenth century (over 400 years ago) that paper money was introduced into Europe. In China they'd actually been using it since AD 650. The reason for this was that metal money was heavy to carry around. Chinese coins were originally given holes in them, because merchants used to string them together so that they didn't lose any. Of course this also meant that if you were robbed, you'd lose the lot in one go!

It must have been very tempting for your average peasant, working away in a field, and seeing this smartly dressed merchant coming along on his horse (camel, bullock, goat, very large frog). It must have been even more tempting and tantalizing to hear all that money jangling around in his pocket, knowing that getting your hands on that cash would probably mean that you never had to work again,[2] and also knowing that there wasn't a policeman for miles around because they hadn't been invented yet. As a result, merchants were often getting robbed. So what could they do about it? Someone – I don't know who – came up with the following idea: merchants would leave their coins with a goldsmith,

2: Money being the universal symbol of wealth and influence.

who would give them a receipt. On the receipt it would say something like:

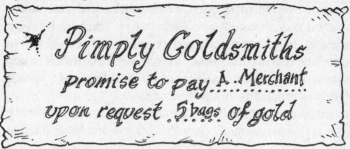

Pimply Goldsmiths promise to pay A. Merchant upon request 5 bags of gold

Travelling light

This idea caught on and was developed so that the merchants could use it to make trips to other countries. Imagine this situation: a merchant from Paris (we'll call him Bill) wants to go to Venice, but he doesn't want to carry any money with him. Fortunately, he knows another Paris merchant (we'll call him Ben) who has an office in Venice. All Bill has to do is give his money to Ben in Paris, who will then give him a receipt. On Bill's arrival in Venice all he has to do is go to Ben's Venice office, show them the receipt and collect his money. And, as long as the merchants trusted each other, the system was foolproof. Unless somebody pinched your receipt.

The bank

As this system developed, silversmiths and goldsmiths started getting together to form banks. The idea was that instead of issuing separate receipts the bank would produce its own receipts, known as "bank notes", each one worth a certain amount of gold. In England this was based on the idea of a pound of gold.[1]

Each bank issued its own banknotes, which must have got very confusing. Eventually this system settled down and central banks were started. The first bank in Europe was the Stockholm Bank in Sweden in 1661. Why Sweden? Well, I suppose the Vikings (who came from Sweden) had made so much money robbing people that they thought they'd better put it safely in the bank, just in case somebody tried to rob *them*!

Each bank note issued by the Bank of Stockholm was worth a hundred *dalers*[2], or silver coins.

The Bank of England

Of course, banknotes in England mostly come from – erm – the Bank of England, which was founded in 1694. I say "mostly" because you can still get pound notes

1: The use of the pound to weigh precious metal dates back to Anglo-Saxon times. A pound of gold was divided up into 240 small coins. These were eventually known as "pennies" and right up until 1971 when decimalization was introduced there were 240 pennies in a pound.
2: Which is probably where dollars comes from.

issued by the Bank of Scotland, and they are perfectly legal in this country – which means that you can still spend them, you'll be pleased to hear. At least, you can if you can get your hands on one before your parents spend it for you!

Incidentally, if you look at a banknote you'll see that it says "I promise to pay the bearer on demand the sum of…" and that sum depends on the note: five pounds, ten, twenty, etc. You'll also notice that the banknote is signed by the chief cashier. What all this means is that if you go into the bank, hand over your banknote and demand £20 (or whatever the note is worth) the bank promises to give you 20 pounds in precious metal. Except that it doesn't. The promise no longer applies.

All the bank will do now is change your £20 into other notes (or coins) worth the same value. They no longer hand over great lumps of gold even though they promise to do so on the note. And it's no good you arguing with them. It's not even worth demanding to see the chief cashier, because a quick check on a number of notes will reveal that it's a different person for each type of note; I've just checked my cash and I've got a fiver signed by C. E. A. Kentfield and a £20 note (that can't be mine!) signed by Merlyn Lowther, who's obviously a much nicer chap and doesn't mind being on first name terms with the rest of us. But try going into the bank and saying: "Can I have a word with Merlyn about getting my hands on 20 pounds of gold?" and see how quickly they show you the door. They just don't do it anymore. I suppose it's just as well really. After all, 20 pounds of gold would be equivalent to carrying ten bags of sugar along the road.[1] No, banks are pretty good but they don't have that much raw gold lying around.

Oh! I've just found a £10 note signed by Elvis Presley. That'll be a forgery then.

The pound in your pocket

So now you know roughly how money started. Obviously buying things is now far more sophisticated than simply handing over cash. For example, there are credit cards, debit cards and electronic banking. You can even pay for things over the phone. But for most of you this is something that you don't really have to think about at the moment – you'll be far more concerned about the cash in your pocket – or the lack of it.

To be honest, the easiest way to keep track of your money is to use cash. And if you're anything like me then keeping track of your money isn't a problem. That's my money over there – those two little round brown things; 3p altogether. But cash is what this book is about, so…

1: 10 two-pound bags obviously!

32

LET'S TALK CASH

Can you remember...

The first time you handled money? I'm not talking about that 5p coin you shoved up your brother's nose, or even the pound coin you swallowed.

WHY DID YOU JUST SWALLOW THAT POUND COIN?

IT WAS "DINNER MONEY"

I swallowed a pound coin when I was little.[1] My mum took me to the doctors and the doctor said that I'd have to wait and it would pass through me. So every morning my mum, being very careful with money, put me on a potty and checked to see if the money had turned up yet, but there was no change.[2]

Probably the first time you handled money was at playschool, although it would have been plastic and smelt of sick. You probably thought: "This money's disgusting. I never want anything to do with it!" Little did you realize then that you would probably spend the rest of your life chasing after money and trying to hang on to it. But then life is strange and cash is even stranger.

Can you remember...

The first time that you were in a shop with your parents, and they handed you a fiver and said: "Give the money to the man, dear." You probably thought: "Do I look like my head zips up at the back? This is the first time I've

1: Which was a clever trick because they didn't have them then.
2: No change! Money – no change! Sorry about that!

ever got my hands on one of these things and I'm hanging on to it." You then promptly screwed it up and poked it in your ear. But this would have been your parents' way of trying to teach you how to pay for something. Strangely enough, the older you get the less keen they are for you to spend money, which doesn't seem right somehow.

Can you remember...

The first time you had some money of your own? You probably can't because you were probably only a few months old. When you get christened, and sometimes when you're born, relatives give you money, which your parents then spend on really hideous clothes for you; the sort of stuff that you'd never be seen dead in if *you* had control of the purse strings. Some relatives give you cheques, which your parents forget to put in the bank for you; or they put them in their own bank account and forget all about them.

Of course, if you're *really* unlucky you get strange things made of silver that are no use to anybody; little trains, Humpty Dumptys and silver spoons with your name, date of birth and other intimate details engraved on them. Years later you find these peculiar gifts, gathering dust in a drawer.

"What's this thing?" You ask your mum.

"Oh, your Uncle David gave you that when you were born."

"That figures," you think to yourself. "He always was a weird one."

Can you remember...

The first time you were actually given money to cope with? It was probably for something at school; school dinners for example. Why anyone should have to pay for the privilege of getting food poisoning beats me. Or maybe it was for school photos, the school trip to the top of the road, or maybe the school were having a collection to try and get the headteacher out of prison.

Whatever the reason, your parents will have pressed a sealed envelope into your hand, saying: "Be careful not to lose it." What a silly thing to say! Obviously you're going to be careful *not* to lose it. What would be the point of being careful *to lose* it? And anyway, money can get lost very easily without any help from you. That's what money's like. One minute it's there, and the next it's gone. That's probably why your parents have sealed the envelope; they're worried about the money trying to escape. Rubbish! They're worried about you nicking it more like! Just imagine: for the first time in your life you've been trusted with an envelope stuffed with dosh. You suddenly realize the truth of the maxim that "money means power" – or in your case independence. You think: "I'll run away!" Great idea! No more getting told off! No more having to go to bed when you're not tired! No more having to get up when you're fast asleep! No more having to have a bath when you hardly smell at all! Brilliant!

Little do you realize that the £3.50 in the envelope is unlikely to get you to the other side of Scunthorpe (even if you live *in* Scunthorpe!) let alone to some paradise island where adults are illegal and the sea tastes of Cola Slush. Actually it's unlikely to be £3.50; it's far more likely to be £3.99, or something that involves your parents struggling to find change in the mad rush-around that is the Monday morning pre-going-to-school panic. They will then find themselves 4p short and be totally convinced that the school "won't have any change". Actually this is a myth devised by schools as a sure-fire money maker. Every time you offer anything other than the right money (which is most times) the school says: "Sorry – no change!" and pockets the difference.

Anyway, having taken most of the furniture apart, ripped up the carpets and performed a tracheotomy on the dog (in case he's swallowed it) they eventually raid your money box.

"Where did you get this £10 note from?" they demand.

"What £10 note?" you enquire, as it disappears into said parent's pocket.

The final outcome is that the required 4p is never found, your £10 note is used to pay the school and the school keeps the change. Still, there is an up side: you get to feel the benefit of your £10 every time it's your turn to use the school pencil. OK, so that's only once a term and it's hardly the same as owning the latest CD by Hunks-R-Us but it could be worse. No, it couldn't!

Can you remember...

The first time somebody gave you money of your *very own*? Money with no strings attached, or even bits of elastic. Oh, Uncle Ivor thinks that's so funny, doesn't he? He turns up every Christmas with a pound coin in his hand; a pound coin that he has carefully drilled a small hole into, and attached a length of elastic to, which is even now running up the inside of his jacket sleeve and is secured in his armpit with an industrial strength safety pin. He proffers the coin to you, saying: "Don't spend it all at once." As you reach forward to take it, assuming that that is what he wants you to do, the coin shoots up his sleeve with the speed of Concorde, cracking three of his ribs in the process. Judging from his laughter he obviously considers this a very small price to pay considering the delight he gets from fooling you – *yet again!* – into thinking that he was going to give you some money. It's a stupid trick but you fall for it; so convinced are you that money will solve all your problems.

Of course, you should have realized that the whole thing was a con the minute he said: "Don't spend it all at once."[1] It is impossible to spend a coin any other way. Consider this: you enter a shop with a pound coin. You want to buy the latest copy of *Birdwatching Monthly*.

1: You should have realized that it was a con the minute he started the whole sorry business. The man's an adult, apparently. And you really should know by now that adult's cannot be trusted. Believe me, I know. I am an adult.

It's got this really interesting article about the pigeons in Trafalgar Square.[1] And the magazine is 50p.[2] You hand over your pound coin, thus *spending it all at once*. OK so you get given change, but the pound coin is gone for ever, unless of course you sneak back later and rob their till, which frankly I've never really thought was a particularly good idea. The coins they give you in change are *different* coins; and also they are coins that you will eventually spend – *all at once*.

But to get back to your Uncle Ivor. (Must we? I suppose we ought to. After all, he's the only one in the family with any money, even if it is all attached to bits of elastic up his sleeve.) If you really want to put him in his place – which by rights would be a secure unit in the middle of Dartmoor – then all you have to say is: "I see you've drilled a hole in this pound coin, Uncle Ivor. Did you realize that the penalty for defacing the coin of the realm is death, followed by a hefty fine?" That's bound to give him a crinkly mouth, and possibly a heart attack; which is only useful if he's made out a will in your favour.

1: OK so I'm talking drivel. I'll get help I promise; just as soon as I finish this book.
2: Ludicrously cheap by most magazine standards, but frighteningly overpriced for this particular publication in my opinion. But then I'm not really into birdwatching. Or at least, I try not to be.

Hang on!

I've just been re-reading this last bit – checking for spelling mistakes, which frankly is a totally pointless exercise for me; my spelling is so bad that I wouldn't spot a mistake if it bit me in the legg. Ouch! No – the thing that caught my attention was not a yet-undiscovered way of spelling *mowth* – sorry *mouth* – it was the phrase *millionaire lunatic*. One of the many things money allows you to be is mad. If you've got buckets of dosh you are allowed to be stark raving bonkers. Take the average popstar – they can go around looking like an explosion in an Oxfam reject bucket, and nobody minds. In fact, people *indulge* them. They can do no wrong. And all because they are *loaded*.

But you try being even a little bit eccentric with those holes in your socks and see where it gets you. Believe me, I've tried it – it doesn't work.

Can you remember...

The first time you were given money for something you had supposedly done? And I'm not talking about the reward you got for shopping the neighbours to the authorities for not having a TV licence.[1] I suppose the sort of thing that I'm thinking about is losing a tooth. That in itself is a contradiction; you don't actually lose it. It comes out. You know exactly where it is; it's embedded in the ear of that kid that everyone hates at playschool. What is odd is that the kid's mum isn't cross with you; in fact she looks delighted. Why is that? you find yourself wondering. But then you stop wondering. After all, you're only three and at three life holds even greater mysteries, such as why do you always start weeing just before you get to the toilet. Odd that, isn't it? Anyway, you get your tooth back – after a bit of a fight which the playgroup leaders seem to be encouraging – and mum says: "Put it under your pillow". Listen – it's hard enough to sleep with those dismembered bits of Action Man and 15 Beanie Babies under the pillow, without the added discomfort of a tooth as well.

When I was little I wanted to marry the Tooth Fairy. If I'm completely honest I still do. After all, anyone who can afford to splash out 50p (or a pound) every time anyone *anywhere* loses a tooth, has got to be *loaded*. Crikey! My mum had all her teeth out in one go.[2] Think

1: Their daughter Mandy illegally taped a Steps CD the other day, if you feel like shopping them again. I think that's probably a crime on two fronts: illegal taping and having a Steps CD in the house.
2: OK so it was a lucky punch. If she'd won she would have been WBA Bantam Weight Champion by now.

of how much that must have set the poor old Tooth Fairy back! But has anyone ever had a note from the Tooth Fairy saying: "Can I settle up with you at the end of the month? I'm a bit short at the moment." Of course they haven't! And who pays the Tooth Fairy's wages? Nobody! She has a private income. I'm telling you, she's loaded. Mind you, if you want to get your hands on her millions you'd have to let her take a large mallet to your teeth, but it would be a small price to pay.[1] I am assuming that the Tooth Fairy is female. There is a reasonable chance that she might be a man, in which case forget that bit about me wanting to marry him; I'll settle for being really good mates and a cash hand-out.

But those first coins that people give you – even the ones from the Tooth Fairy – they're really special, aren't they? You hold them; you don't want to let them go. To you they're not really money; they're something magical. Sounds silly? Not really. Money is magical; it can disappear so fast that you don't even know it's gone.

Can you remember...

The first time you were given pocket money? Ah, pocket money; blood money more like. Pocket money is one of the ways that parents control their children. There are

1: This is a very old expression. Frankly, these days there is no such thing as a small price to pay.

lots of others, but pocket money is one of the least subtle ways. Does any of this look familiar?

Car cleaning and pocket money should be totally separate issues. In fact, pocket money shouldn't be related to household chores at all. But more of this later.

But do you remember the time when you started getting pocket money on a regular basis? I'm not talking about your parent grudgingly handing over a handful of small coins – most of them foreign – because you've demanded the much-promised regular pocket money. I'm talking about a regular, never-missed weekly ritual involving your parent(s) willingly placing an agreed sum into your hand with no strings, no elastic and no very small print; money that is yours to do with as you please.

Yes, you're right – that will probably *never* happen! But suppose it does. Oh come on, we can dream can't we? Just suppose that for some reason you do find yourself in possession of money that is yours to do with

1: Actually there's no such thing as "the car". That means my car. Parents like to try to pretend that their car is in some way the family vehicle – but try offering to drive and see how far it gets you.

as you please. Maybe your parent has had an adult personality by-pass or something. Anyway, whatever the reason, here you are with a fistful of dosh that is yours and yours alone. You're on the town and *loaded*. Do you seriously think your parent is going to let you make such a big decision as how to spend your pocket money *on your own*? Think again! There's this CD you fancy. Just as you are about to take it to the counter they appear at your elbow and say: "Hmm, yes dear. Not a *bad* choice. But for 50p less you can get this triple album of *Cliff Richard's Greatest Hits*." You look at it. Sure, it's got everything he's ever done on it. It's even got a rocking little number that got him banned from the court of King Harold, back in 1065. In fact, if William the Conqueror hadn't won at Hastings, Cliff might have vanished into obscurity.

As you toy with the CD in your hand, your parent is still wittering on.

"The point is that this fab new boy band/girl band will be forgotten by next week, but Cliff will live on for ever."

There's certainly evidence to back up the second part of this opinion.

"But I can't stand Cliff Richard," you whimper, already feeling that the battle might be lost. Moments later you are walking out of the store, CD dangling in a gossamer-thin plastic bag that is not only totally non-biodegradable but also emits toxic fumes. Through the plastic curtain that is the side of the bag, the entire world (plus all of your mates) can clearly read *Cliff Richard's Greatest Hits – a Millennium of Masterly Music*. The up side is that by saving yourself 50p, you had just enough money to buy a set of earplugs, so it wasn't a totally wasted journey.

This has been just one short journey into the murky world of buying and selling. There will be many, many more. And it won't get any easier.

Money is power

You probably remember that I mentioned this earlier. If you don't then it doesn't matter; you don't need to go back and check. More than any other thing, money can be used to manipulate people. We've already touched on the kind of moral blackmail that parents use to control you by threatening to withhold money for jobs not done, or offering cash inducements for jobs they want you to do. Nowhere will you feel this more keenly than when you go on a family holiday.[1]

Wish you weren't here

Just imagine the situation: you've scrimped and saved for months; you've carefully salted away your pocket money, despite the fact that there have been loads of things you wanted to buy: computer games, CDs, tapes, sweets, the list is endless. Finally, the holiday date looms and you have managed to save up enough money to ensure a totally cool time. It hasn't been easy. You've had

1: "Family holiday" is a strange expression. The only thing that ever really ruins a family holiday is having your family with you!

to toss aside your principles in the pursuit of cash. You've done extra jobs around the house, you've made your bed without being asked, you've been nice to your little brother, you've gone a whole week without arguing with your sister, you've cleaned out your rabbit's hutch, eaten all your peas, done your homework and even tidied your room! Heck – if you were on proper wages you'd be a multi-millionaire after doing all that lot.[1] And so, after the long car journey with all the obligatory holiday journey features such as getting lost, community singing, throwing up, saying: "Are we there yet?" and the car blowing up, you finally reach your holiday destination – Powerstation-By-The-Sea.

OK, so it doesn't look too special, but you quickly suss the fact that there are things to do – on top of which there's this girl/boy that's staying in the same hotel. Yes. This could turn into the holiday of a lifetime – just as long as the cash holds out. Because cash is the only way

1: Yes, I appreciate that these jobs wouldn't normally generate cash, but this is the lead up to holidays and parents are known to be more generous around about this time, aren't they? Aren't they? Oh – maybe that's where I'm going wrong!

that you are going to be able to keep yourself independent of the rest of the family. With enough of the folding stuff tucked in your back pocket you'll be able to go your own way and nobody can stop you.

Oh you think so, do you? Think again. Parents on holiday have ways of making sure that you stay totally dependent on them, and therefore within telling-off range. So how do they do it? Very easily as it happens. On the first day of the holidays you all climb into your matching plastic macs – yes! It's raining! Wouldn't you know it!

What makes it even more annoying is the fact that the last two weeks of term witnessed a heat wave. One child was actually microwaved because he was wearing an acrylic blazer. But the minute the holidays arrive it's torrential downpours all round. You secretly hope that the school might get washed away in a flash flood – but it won't.

Anyway – there you are, looking like the Von Trapp family singers,[1] walking into the nearest souvenir shop to get gifts for those relatives who haven't had the good fortune to be on holiday (or misfortune depending on how you look at it). Parents always insist that cards and gifts are bought on the first day. As a child I used to think

1: From *The Sound of Music*. What do you mean you've never seen it – where do you go every Christmas?

that this was because the rest of the fortnight would be so stuffed with excitement that we wouldn't have time within our heady schedule to squeeze in even two minutes of card-buying.

"And don't forget to buy something nice for Granny," your mum warns, knowing that she'll never hear the last of it if you don't.

And so you buy postcards for everybody; relatives, neighbours, pets, neighbours' pets, relatives' pets, neighbours' relatives, relatives' neighbours, neighbours' relatives' pets, relatives' neighbours' pets, neighbours' pets' neighbours' relatives' pets. Friends. Friends' pets. Pets' friends… Oh, I think you get the idea! Anyway – back at the "hotel", a badly converted abattoir, you take stock of your new financial position. Broke. Penniless. So what are you going to do for cash for the rest of the fortnight? Offer protection to your little brother in return for cash?[1] Forget it! He's even broker than you are, having blown all his cash on a large plastic turtle, which he just *had* to have. Once you return home – assuming that you all survive that long – the turtle will have pride of place in a hastily-put-together aquatic display involving Action Man exploring some bits of lettuce,

1: Protection from you, obviously – as in "Pay up or I'll thump you!"

dressed in a state-of-the-art diving suit made from a washing-up bottle and loo rolls. By this time next month the turtle will have become a forgotten dust-gatherer who lives under the bed. None of which solves your current financial situation, which is desperate. And that gorgeous girl/boy is waving at you right now! The fact is that you will spend the next two weeks walking six paces behind your parents, looking like an MI6 agent stalking two escaped lunatics. Dad will be wearing a T-shirt with "I'm with this idiot" emblazoned across the front, and an arrow pointing at mum, who will be wearing a T-shirt which reads "Girl Having Fun!" – a statement that nobody will believe for a minute. Your entertainment will be entirely governed by what your parents want to do; which might be fine except they want to visit the Big Fish Centre which seems to consist of a small tank with a goldfish in it. The goldfish looks like it's been inflated with a bicycle pump to make it look bigger. Oh, and they also want to visit the local Co-op, because it's a bit bigger than the one you've got at home. Unlike you, your parents will be having the time of their lives, *doing things as a family*.

As if you don't do that all year round. After all, you all live, eat, sleep and go to the loo in the same house, don't you? You even talk to each other occasionally without being prompted.[1] What more do these people want?

By Tuesday you're desperate. You've just spent the morning watching Little Brother break the world record for the number of goes on a half-inflated bouncy castle. Unfortunately the man from the *Guinness Book of Records* wasn't there to witness it, but don't worry – dad's shot three rolls of film of it, so you should be able to make your own flicker book of the momentous event. It's about now that you hear yourself whinge:

Yes! Your parents hold the purse strings and so they are going to control everything, including your ice-cream consumption. But why are they doing it? Don't they want you to have a good time? Of course they do! But you don't have to spend money to have a good time, apparently. After all, think of all the lovely fresh air you're getting wandering around like the Lost Tribe of Anorak. And it isn't costing you a penny! Mainly because you haven't got one.

1: Mealtimes are the worst. Dad tells you to turn the radio off so that you can all have a decent conversation, and then the minute you try to start one he tells you off for talking whilst you're eating. You can't win – but then you probably already knew that!

Of course, the real truth behind this situation is far more sinister. Your parents won't be able to relax and enjoy the holiday unless they know exactly what you're up to morning, noon and night (and all the times in between). The only way to achieve this is to make sure that you are totally dependent on them. And by making sure that you have no money of your own, they achieve exactly what they have set out to do.

And of course, it doesn't stop at holidays. There are lots of ways that parents use cash to control you. For instance:

Enjoy your trip

Yes! The good old school trip. Even if it's just a quick visit to the park with a bunch of other mixed-up infants, your parents have still had to cough up £2.50 towards the gallons of gnat-bite cream that Mrs Eavesdrop the headteacher will need to stop her being eaten alive by small insects who don't have the intelligence to know that she's poisonous.

WHY ARE YOU STANDING IN A PILE OF DEAD GNATS, MISS?

As you leave home that morning your mum issues a veiled threat; so veiled in fact that you probably don't even realize that it *is* a threat:

"Now be on your best behaviour. This trip has cost me a lot of money."

You can tell that it is in some way special. After all, you're being allowed to wear your own clothes. Little do you know that this is due to the fact that the school came to the conclusion many years ago that it wasn't safe to take the children out of school in uniform because they were too easily identifiable. It's much easier for teachers to disown the children in their care if they aren't wearing uniform, especially if the little dears have just set fire to somebody as they did in 1987.

To make matters worse, the children sat around the blaze singing campfire songs they'd learned at Beavers, only with different words. Yes – probably not the ideal time to be wearing uniform to be honest; not that *you*'ll cause any trouble.

You're too sensible for one thing.[1] For another thing you have had the idea firmly planted in your head that one false move on your part and any further trips could be off the menu. OK, so it's only the park now – but once you get to secondary school you could be jetting off to really exotic places, like the ancient trumping mines in Widgett-on-the-Marsh. Or skiing in Canada.

Wow! That's a biggy. And don't your parents know it.

1: Sorry – I didn't mean to call you sensible. After all, you wouldn't be reading this book if you were that sensible, would you?

They've been scratching[1] and saving for months so that you can go. Why are they so keen? Are they planning to move while you're away? No! They want you to enjoy yourself. Not too much, obviously, but they won't mind if you watch a bit of Canadian TV, or pay a cultural visit to Niagara Falls. But they start to work on you the minute the list of things you'll need comes through from school. And what a list! Why do you need 17 sweaters – you're only going for a week? Surely even Canada can't be that cold, can it?

Maybe this is the list for the entire school party, which for some reason your parents have been elected to provide. If they had the slightest inkling about your parents' appalling fashion sense they would never have bothered. Anyway, your parents take you off to the ski shop where they start playing that game that all parents are really good at: appearing very generous by offering to buy you a skiing outfit, and then spoiling it totally by insisting on buying the only one in the shop that nobody – not even Eddie "The Eagle" Edwards – would be seen dead in.[2] And the further down the list you go, the worse everything gets.

1: The scratching has got nothing to do with money – the dog's infested with fleas again.
2: Eddie "The Eagle" Edwards was the only British person ever to do any good in the Winter Olympics skiing events. And even he did really, really badly. Which probably goes to prove that skiing just isn't this country's thing – along with football, cricket, golf, eating, walking, talking, etc.

"Will he/she really need sun block? It *is* rather expensive." your parent ventures tentatively.

"Yes, unless you *want* them to come home looking as though they've been involved in a nuclear accident."

A long pause for thought from your parent. They're surely not seriously considering this as a possibility are they? And then comes the warning:

"Well, take care and make it last. You could use it for cleaning your teeth as well. It has got a minty smell."

This continues with every item purchased, until you are standing amid a small mountain of neatly wrapped packages. You have been treated to a mountain of very expensive gear; you've also been treated to what your parent considers to be subtlety. But the message is very clear: my money went into this stuff, so mess about and you won't be able to move for the mountain of guilt that will crash down on your head. Actually, mess around on the ski slope and you probably won't be able to move for the plaster around your broken limbs, but that's another story.

Once more from the top

But if you think that money-based parental manipulation stops there, think again! Remember those piano lessons?[1] Great, weren't they? OK, so you weren't a natural pianist. It took you three lessons to realize the

1: Or was it keyboard? I can't remember.

piano lid was down. Why didn't your piano teacher point that out? Simple – she was charging by the hour, and the longer it took you to get the lid open the more she got paid. It soon became obvious, even to your parents, that as far as the piano was concerned you were no Vanessa-Mae. (Which is just as well, because she plays the violin.) Because of this your parents have opted to pay for one lesson at a time, and so the weekly ritual is as follows:

1. You tuck your piano music under your arm ready to leave the house for your lesson.

I BET BEETHOVEN DIDN'T HAVE THIS TROUBLE!

2. You tuck the piano under the other. No! Only joking! You drag the piano on a small trolley behind you.
3. You stand in front of your parent in a sad pose that means: Can I have the money for my lesson, please?

Your parent then goes into a whole routine destined to make you feel:

A. Guilty that you're not a child genius.
B. Very, very humbled that your parents would go without important things like chocolate so that you can have a musical education.

Unfortunately, this doesn't work because you never wanted piano lessons in the first place. Not that you're not interested in music; you are. But you've failed to find anyone who teaches paper and comb.

But the underlying message is clear; this is moral blackmail plain and simple. In exactly the same way as you dared not put a foot wrong on the school trip for fear of letting your parents (and their money) down, so you bash away at the piano simply because your parents are paying for you to do so. Actually, bashing the piano could be where you're going wrong; you're meant to hit those black and white things in some kind of order, not in batches of six.

By now I'm sure you can see how this parental-control-via-money thing works, and you can apply it to almost any situation that you find yourself in where money is an issue:

OK, so that last one may not be such a good example, but I'm sure you get the idea. Actually the pen one is a bit suspect too. And I don't think the excuse "Sorry I haven't done my homework, Sir, only my mum refused to buy me a new pen" cuts a lot of ice with most teachers.

The curse of the coin

So is that what money's about? Salt, feathers and bits of old metal that parents use to control you? Of course it isn't! It's far more complicated than that. So far I've just scratched the surface. To be honest, it would take a book the size of Cornwall to corner all the mysteries of money.

I imagine that you're starting to feel that life would be a lot simpler if we didn't have to bother about money at all. Well done! You're absolutely right! Unfortunately, virtually everything we do involves money at one point or another, and so we actually can't live without it. So all we can do is learn to *cope*. And that's why I'm here! Have I ever let you down in the past? Of course not! Probably. So hold my hand and let me steer you through the complex world of cash. But be warned – it's going to be a bumpy journey!

THE A-Z OF COPING WITH CASH

What follows is a guide to some of the many facets of cash; the pitfalls and the problems, but also the joys and delights. In order to make it more manageable I've arranged the various headings into cunningly simple, user-friendly alphabetical order. And to make things even simpler I'm going to start with "A":

Accountant

What is it?
Look around your classroom. Go on – the teacher won't mind. Teachers like to see their pupils moving, it proves that they're still awake (and alive!). The kid over there who's especially good at maths – can you see her? Well one day she could quite easily be an accountant. But what exactly is it? Well, basically it's somebody who does accounts, although I expect you'd worked that much out for yourself. If you earn a lot of money – or if you're just useless with money (like I am!) – then you might need to hire an accountant to manage it for you. Don't worry, it's unlikely that you're going to need one to manage your pocket money for you, unless you're very lucky, or your parents are even worse with money than I am. But as you get older and start earning, an accountant will keep records of everything you spend and everything you earn; they'll sort out things like income tax for you, and generally help you handle your cash. Pop stars usually have armies of accountants working for them, and their job is to invest the pop star's money and hope-fully make more money for him/her. Again, this is not something you'll need, so why am I telling you? Well, remember when you took those home-made biscuits into school? Everybody said how tasty they were and

could you bring in some more. So what did you do? You made more and sold them in little bags for a pound, didn't you? Great idea; very enterprising.

And you might still be doing it now if that smart kid who knows everything hadn't spotted the fact that they were dog biscuits coated in icing sugar. Huh! Some kids are just too bright for their own good, aren't they? It makes me sick, it really does! Anyway, if Smartypants hadn't rumbled your scam, your home-made biscuit empire would have grown and grown, the money would have been rolling in and you would have needed help to sort it all out. And that's where an accountant would have come in handy.

How to cope
There's not much to cope with. An accountant will cope for you. Finding a good one is the tricky part!

Bank account
What is it?
This is the thing that the bank keeps people's money in. I did a bit of checking, which involved disguising myself as a very small child (if you've ever seen me you'll realize

just how tricky that was!) and going into the bank with a fistful of *Monopoly* money. At first, they thought I was a very short bank robber and the cashier pressed the panic button.

I must say that the police were very understanding, and once the tear gas had cleared we were able to have a good laugh about it, until the hospital sister told us that laughing wasn't allowed in Intensive Care. However, I'm now pretty well over the shock, and I did find out the following:[1]

You can open a bank account in your own name at 7. This surprised me because I thought that banks didn't open until 9.30. Then I realized that they meant 7 years old. You can have an account in a parent's name before you're 7, but if you want to be able to get your hands on your cash without them interfering (fat chance!) then you need to be 7, which I'm sure you are, even if you don't look it.[2] To take your money out of the account you just go into the bank, ask, and they'll give you your cash. But you must be able to prove who you are. It's no

1: This information may vary from bank to bank. I went to Barclays. Mainly because they've got my money (in a sock under the manager's bed).

2: It's worth mentioning that if your parents open an account for you before you are 7, they can help themselves to your cash without you knowing – so be warned!

good saying: "Hand over my dosh – the Telebubbies have got the place surrounded," even if they have. Banks are not impressed by that sort of thing.

Of course, keeping your money safely in the bank is not going to stop your parents getting their hands on it. For all you know the bank manager might even help them; after all, he or she is probably a parent too!

How to cope
Keep your money in a sock under the bed. But make sure that the sock is locked inside your money box.[1] Better still, spend your money so you won't have to worry about losing it.

Birthday money

What is it?
This is the best kind of money because it is all yours, to do whatever you want with. That's the theory, anyway. In practice it rather depends on when you were born. I was born in the middle of August, for instance. Not only did this mean that I'd had a year less in infant school than

1: See also MONEY BOX

most of my mates, but it also meant that I was almost certainly going to fall victim to the massive Back to School campaign that all the high street shops mount at around the middle of August. Maybe it was my sad lack of education, or maybe I just wasn't as sharp as other kids, but the minute the birthday money fell out of the envelope my mum was saying "You need new school shoes" and I was agreeing with her.[1]

I say that the minute the money arrived the shoe conversation took place, but that's not strictly true. The minute the money fell out of the envelope the Thank You letter conversation took place.[2]

Now, possibly I can be forgiven for believing that once we got to the shoe shop I would be allowed to pick my own new shoes. After all, it was my birthday, and my birthday money. Not at all. Or at least, not exactly. I *was* allowed to try on the latest fashions but amazingly none of them fitted.

"We just don't seem to have your size in the winkle-picker elastic-sided Chelsea boot,[3] sir," the assistant purred.

It wasn't until years later that I realized that my mum and the assistant were in league. After all, they were both from the same planet – Planet Parent – and so they were bound not to understand. Ironically, whenever I try the same trick on my own children I get the 12-year-old work-experience assistant who comes from the same planet as my kids – Planet Cool – and so I wind up spending a fortune on trainers and getting hauled up in front of my son's headmaster to explain his "inappropriate footwear". Listen mate – all I did was pay for them!

1: See also UGLY SHOES
2: See also THANK YOU LETTERS
3: Yes I know they sound awful now, but I thought they were to die for. I did eventually get some and I've had foot trouble ever since, partly because my feet are now pointed.

How to cope

If you find yourself being forced to spend your birthday money on ugly shoes, then there may be a way out of it. When you and mum first go into the shop, insist on trying on the shoes you really want, but don't argue when she says that you can't have them because they're not suitable for school. Put the shoes to one side but make sure that the assistant doesn't put them away. You can achieve this by quickly picking the ugliest shoes you can find.

Put these on and then walk around the shop saying "Wow, Mummy, I really love *these* shoes. They're much nicer than those other ones. I'm only sad that I haven't got enough money to buy two pairs!" Try to say this in that syrupy sweet way that only kids on American TV shows can really do. If you can also manage to walk in a strange dream-like fashion that might help.

You want to give the impression that the shoes have in some way turned you into the Nicest Person In The World, possibly even The Universe. Start to sing with joy – badly, obviously. If you can manage to get a few other customers to run out of the shop screaming, so much the better. Mum will probably say:

"Well, if you like them that much maybe I could pay for a second pair."

63

The extra pairs of shoes are kept in another room, possibly even the cellar. The assistant will not want to leave the shop with you behaving like a demented Shirley Temple,[1] and so she'll say:

"Sorry, that's the last pair. But actually I don't think these are too bad."

At this point she'll pick up the fashion shoes that you originally tried on, in a bustling "Shall I wrap these up? Don't dare say no." sort of way that comes with years of shoe-shop-assistant training, and bingo! You get the shoes you want, paid for with your own money, and mum (or dad) gets the pleasure of buying you sensible (but ugly) shoes with their own money. Sorted! – as they say (all the time) on *EastEnders*.[2]

Book token[3]

What is it?

This is a form of money. But, unlike other forms you can only buy a book with it. Although it is commonly known as a book token, its full name is "Oh no! What can I get them for Christmas/birthday? I know I'll give them a book token." Although, in fairness, it has to be said that many people like books, and even like getting them as presents. I always buy a load of books as presents for people at Christmas and then wind up keeping most of them myself. I love books, but then I also write them.[4] But sometimes the joy of owning a book is picking it yourself. And in this instance a book token is the perfect

---

1: Shirley Temple was an American child star who could make anyone sick without trying. She's now a politician, so no change there then.

2: For any foreigners reading this book – welcome to the English language. *EastEnders* is a TV programme in which things (and people) get sorted regularly, and then other people (and things) talk about it.

3: See also GIFT TOKEN

4: Did you realize that I wrote books? It may not be that obvious from reading this!

gift. But suppose that you've been given a book token for your birthday or Christmas, but you don't want to buy a book. Or more to the point, there's something you want much, much more, but no amount of hinting has managed to get the idea through to any of your relatives.[1] So instead of the latest *Great Pink Wobbly Things* CD – which is brilliant if you like middle-of-the-road Hip Hop – or the latest PC game *Clam Throbbing Beats Off the Graphically Challenged Alien Hordes Single-handedly III* – which is also brilliant if you like blood-spattered body parts and ballerinas – you open up your birthday card and get – wow! – a book token!

How to cope

So how do you turn this limited currency into hard cash, without offending anyone? Well, you could try saying: "Oh, a book token! Lovely! But I think I've already read this one." You could try that but it's unlikely to work. If you're an identical twin and your twin has been given cash then you could try saying to your twin: "I think this is for you. People are always getting us mixed up." This is also unlikely to work. If you can't actually con anyone into exchanging it for money, then your best hope is to find two shops; one which sells CDs and computer

1: Don't worry – relatives have this problem. It's called selective deafness and it usually means that they don't want you to have it.

games and a few books, which for the sake of argument we'll call *Smith's*; and a bookshop that accepts book tokens, which we'll call *Jones's*. Then what you do is use your token to buy a book in *Jones's*. You then take it into *Smith's* and say:

"A relative bought this book for me as a present but I've already got it. Can I exchange it for another book?"

"Of course you can," beams the assistant.[1]

"Thank you," you reply.

Then you have a quick look round their (unimpressive) book selection. You then go back to the assistant.

"Oh dear," you say, looking glum, "you don't appear to have any book that I could allow myself to be seen reading. I wonder if I could have a refund?"

"Oh dear…" stutters the assistant, quietly thinking that making this difficult decision could be more that their job is worth.

"I know," you say, helpfully, "I could take a computer game instead, even though I'd much rather have a book you understand."

"Of course!" blurts out the rather relieved assistant.

You select your game and go back to the counter.

"I'll take this one. Maybe I could have it a bit cheaper as I don't really want it and will probably never play it."

No! I think we could be pushing our luck!

Bribes

What are they?
Bribes are sums of money paid to somebody else in order to get them to do something. Occasionally, they are sums of money paid to somebody in order to get them *not* to do something, although this is usually called blackmail. Since I haven't done a separate entry on

1: They do that in Smith's; a bit too much for my liking.

blackmail I'd better quickly cover it here: suppose you'd done something that you didn't want your parents to find out about. In a fit of remorse, when you were feeling weighed down with the burden of guilt, you accidentally told your smaller brother/sister about your "crime", which actually wasn't that serious. Although it might have been; after all, you know what you've done, I don't! Anyway, little brother/sister decides that a very good way to make a bit of cash is to threaten to "tell" unless you cough up so much a week. Horrible or what? Of course, it wouldn't be so bad if you'd thought of it first, but still it is a terrible thing to do to a sibling. After all, you're both on the same side, battling against the alien parent hordes. Anyway, this sort of thing is called blackmail.[1] What you threaten to do to your brother/sister if they ever tell is called Attempted Murder!

Let's get back to bribery, it's much nicer. There are many, many forms of bribery in society; businessmen give councillors or politicians gifts, holidays, etc., in return for contracts that will make them more cash. Nothing quite like that exists within the bosom of the family. OK, so your parent might say "I'll give you a fiver if you clean my car".[2] But that could be just a straight business deal.[3] It only really becomes bribery if you just don't want to clean the car. So yes, it's always bribery!

1: Which is neither clever nor funny. It's also illegal; so please don't do it!
2: And pigs might fly.
3: See also JOBS

How to cope

Bribery is a dirty word. So is mud. But it can be turned to your advantage.[1] The big difference between bribery and wages is that with bribery the stakes are usually higher. The trick is to make sure that things you are asked to do never become jobs. Jobs have a fixed rate payment, whereas if you're asked to do something, you can make it seem like a one-off event. But you've got to be clever. The scenario goes something like this:

"Can you give my car a clean?"

"Sorry Dad/Mum/whoever you are. I'm doing my homework."

"No, you're not. You're sitting there doing nothing."

"That's my homework. I've got to see how long I can sit here doing nothing. I'm timing myself."

"We never had anything like that when I was at school."

"No. This is new. It's called social studies. It's replaced corporal punishment as part of the National Curriculum."

"Oh."

There'll now probably be quite a long pause while your parent gets their head around the great leaps that education has taken – not always forwards unfortunately – since they were at school. You'll probably hear all this whirring around in your parent's head. Don't be alarmed. New ideas often settle noisily into adult brains.

1: Bribery can – not mud.

Eventually:

"If you clean the car I'll give you a pound."

Note that the goal posts have moved. The Parent now expects the car to be cleaned – actually cleaned clean – for a pound!

"Isn't there a minimum wage?" you think but don't say. I'll explain why in a minute. What you actually say is:

"Two pounds. Three."

"Sorry – I'm busy."

"Oh come on – it won't take five minutes!"

FIVE?!? Two and a half, tops!

"I'll give you a fiver."

It's at this point that you have to play a very careful game. It's exactly like chess only without the board or the pieces or the... Actually it's nothing like chess at all. But it is tricky. One of the things you *mustn't* say is:

"A fiver? Wow! I'll clean it every week for a fiver!"

But then you probably realized that!

The best approach is to give a huge sigh as you appear to break your concentration.

"Oh dear," you sigh, "I'm going to have to start this project all over again! I might as well clean the car. A fiver you said? OK – just this once."

Try and get the money up front. Impossible I know, but try, because if you don't, then getting the money will be:

a) dependent on how well you do the job, which you already know is going to be *badly*.

And…

b) impossible.

If your younger sibling comes out while you're cleaning the car and hangs about asking tricky car-cleaning related questions, such as "Aren't you going to put any water in your bucket?" then this is almost certainly your parent's idea of quality control. Another very good reason for making sure you get the money up front. Otherwise this will happen:

Yes! Little siblings can be relied on to shop you every time. Unless, of course, you bribe them first.

But why do I insist that you should make sure that this is a one-off and not a regular date with a sponge, bucket and car? I would have thought that that was obvious. If you strike a car-cleaning deal with your parent on a once-a-week-five-pounds-a-time basis then:

a) You'll be stuck doing it every week whether you want to or not.

b) You'll never improve on the price because your parent will say: "You agreed a fiver!" and no amount of saying "But that was 20 years ago!" will make any difference.

Bus pass

What is it?

An important part of school life, especially for those of you who go to school by bus, is the bus pass.[1] As the name suggests, it's a pass that allows you to travel on the bus without paying. This is because your bus fare has already been paid by your parent when they paid for the pass. The pass is proof of this payment in much the same way as a banknote is proof that the bank will give you that amount of precious metal, even though they won't. But unlike a banknote, a bus pass is worth its weight in gold.[2] It's the difference between getting home or being cast into schoolchild wilderness, forced to wander for ever carrying a very heavy bag wearing ugly shoes. Try boarding the bus without your pass and see how right I am. Even if the driver knows you personally:

"Hello, Driver."

"Oh hello, Young Child That I Know Personally. How are you today?"

"Fine – except that I've lost my bus pass."

"But it's me! Young Child That You Know Personally. I travel on your bus every day."

"Not without a pass you don't! How would it be if I let every Tom, Dick and Harry on to the bus without a pass?"

1: A totally unimportant part of school life for those of you who don't, but stick with it!

2: Actually, bus passes are so light and flimsy, that they are probably literally worth their weight in gold.

He pauses to greet a few of your school mates (and check their passes):

Then he turns to you:

"You still here? Hop it!"

"But how am I going to get home?"

"That's not my problem. You can go by bus if you pay the fare."

"But I've got a bus pass."

"Let's see it."

"I've lost it."

How to cope

The simple answer is never lose your bus pass, but that's easier said than done. Bus passes are made from a special material that is noted for its lose-ability. A bus pass can be chained to a block of concrete in the glare of search-lights and security cameras and still disappear. The great magician and escapologist Harry Houdini was made of bus pass material. Unfortunately, Paul Daniels isn't. None of which solves your problem. Sorry. I suppose all we can hope is for bus drivers who realize that, if a person travels on the bus every day of their life using a bus pass, and then suddenly says "I've lost it" they are probably telling the truth. After all, who in their right mind would want to lie in order to travel on a bus, other than an escaped lunatic?

Maybe the driver thinks he's carrying a load of fair-dodging escaped lunatics! That's worrying. But even more worrying is the fact that he doesn't really see you, he only sees the pass; and with that dangerous level of short-sightedness they've put him in charge of a bus! Now that *is* scary!

Cash

What is it?
Well, I think we've established exactly what it is. The reason that I've included it in this A-Z is to remind me to tell you to always insist on cash. Preferably up front. Parents will sometimes try to get you to do things for bits of cake or an extra half an hour before bedtime.

CLEAN OUT THE CAT TRAY AND YOU CAN HAVE THIS BOILED SWEET I FOUND IN MY COAT POCKET

OOOH, HOW TEMPTING

Take the money; you can buy your own cake, and you never go to sleep when you go to bed anyway so half an hour's not going to mean anything!

How to cope
Read this book. Simple enough for you?

Debt

What is it?
If you borrow money that you then can't pay back, you are said to be "in debt". A typical situation that you are likely to find yourself in is this: you're out shopping for something sensible with your parent(s). You see something that is definitely not sensible, but really *cool* and you simply *must* have it.

But you're a bit strapped for cash. In fact, you haven't got any. But you can't let a little thing like no money stop you. After all, it's only £10. So what do you do? You go:
    "Mum – can you lend me £10? I'll pay you back."
    A bit of a rash promise I know, but you're desperate.
    "All right – but make sure you do."
    Wow! This woman is a saint. Can she really be your mum? Anyway, you get the cash, buy the thing, making sure not to wave it about in mum's face too much; after all, she's not likely to appreciate why you think it's so *cool* because she's a parent.
    Your joy is complete. It's easy to forget that you are in debt to the tune of £10, and to a woman who never forgets *anything*. Crikey, she can even tell you which

74

Coronation Street character was the first one to have their brain removed.[1] So she's bound to remember something as momentous as lending you money.

How to cope

The first thing to do is never mention the money ever, not even in passing or as a joke. Comments like: "That's the last you've seen of that £10" are definitely a bad idea. You should be able to tell when mum is building up to asking for her money back, because parents don't understand subtlety. When you notice this happening, you go into action: start leaving things around the dining room (if you're anything like us, the dining room is probably the kitchen). The sort of thing I'm thinking about is a sock, a magazine, a bit of Lego; things that in themselves are not too noticeable. But after a week of dumping things, quite a pile will have built up, although because it's spread around the room it'll probably be only mildly irritating.

Once you've built up a decent collection, move the whole lot into the middle of the dining table and retreat to the bathroom.

DO-BEE -DO...

1: And not have it replaced with acting talent unfortunately.

After a very short time you should hear a minor explosion; this will be the sound of your mum reaching the end of her tether. Fix your face in an expression of concern – checking in the bathroom mirror will help you achieve this – and then head downstairs. Stroll into the dining room/kitchen and say:

"Everything all right, Mum? You haven't seen my left sock, have you?"

"If it was on the table then it's in the bin."

Change your concerned expression to one of horror as you take in – apparently for the first time – the fact that the entire contents of the dining table have disappeared.

"Oh no!" you cry, confident that an Oscar award is waiting round the corner. "The £10 that I owe you was in among that lot!"

A number of things could now happen:

1. Mum could say: "Oh dear. Well, it's my fault. I'll never see that again." And your debt will be wiped out.
2. Mum may immediately head for the dustbin and start raking through it.

If this happens, then it might be a good idea to start telling her about the project you're doing at school on the Black Death. You could point out the fact that it spread and ultimately killed half of Europe due to the amount of rubbish lying in the streets and back gardens; not to mention kitchen/dining room tables. That should stop her.

3. It's possible that while you're discussing the problem, the bin men might arrive and take away the offending rubbish without anyone hearing them. This is very likely; bin men are as nifty as ninjas when it comes to rubbish removal. If this happens your mum might say: "Oh well, you did your best to pay me back, dear. It's my own silly fault that I lost the money."

4. The absolute favourite situation is 3., but instead of mum admitting defeat, she complains very loudly to the local council refuse department, even threatening to tell the local newspapers;[1] even the local TV company. The refuse department will "refund" the £10, and maybe a little bit more besides, without batting an eyelid. Well, actually they might bat an eyelid, or even two, although flirting is not an essential part of customer relations.

In this last scenario everybody wins; mum gets her £10, you get to hang on to yours and the local council get to pride themselves on their high standard of customer care.

1: You may have to suggest this; mum will never think of it on her own.

I suppose the only slight down side is that what you would be doing is technically fraud, and therefore illegal.

Earnings

See JOBS

Errands

What are they?

An errand is usually when you go somewhere for someone. To the shops when one of your parents has run out of something, for instance.

"Oh no! There's no jam! Nip up the corner shop for me, would you?"

This is, of course, a great opportunity to practise your bribery skills.

"Well, yes I would but I need to clean my school shoes."

In this instance, you have to be sure that cleaning your shoes was not something that you'd told your parents that you'd already done the night before. But it has to be said that most parents are particularly gullible when it comes to things like clean shoes:

Even if they don't approve, no parent likes to think that they're out of fashion; it's a sign of old age.[1]

The problem with errands is that they usually involve words like "nip" and "pop". By which I mean that they are fast things; things done in a hurry. And like most things done in a hurry there's not a lot of room for negotiation. So long-winded and subtle ploys are out of the question.

How to cope

Listen out for phrases like "You can keep the change." These are the key to a successful errand. Of course, a bit of nudging might be required; even a blatant "Can I keep the change?" although that might be too obvious. No, probably not – after all we are talking about parents, aren't we? They're not noted for being able to see through a blag, even though they were once young themselves.[2] Having extracted the key phrase by whatever method (try "Did you say 'keep the change?'" that might work), you head off up the shop. Now if you want to make the maximum profit out of the trip, you return with only half the things on the list; this whole venture was thrown together in a blind panic, so you can be forgiven for not remembering everything.

I'M SURE THERE'S SOMETHING MISSING

OOOH, ONLY ABOUT HALF OF IT!

1: Of course, what they don't realize is that when you actually do get old you don't give a stuff about fashion. Not that I'd know about that; I'm far too young!
2: Hard to believe, I know – but it was only once. Probably a Thursday.

Or you could try the "They didn't have any" ploy. But be careful:

"Where's my newspaper?"

"They didn't have any."

"But they're a newsagent's!"

Yes! Be careful! Now comes the moment of truth:

"Where's my change?"

"You told me to keep it."

"Oh yes."

Again, be careful; coming back from the shops having bought nothing and then expecting to keep the change is probably pushing it, just a bit. But then again, you know your own parents better than I do.

Exchange rates

What are they?

If you travel abroad you have to change your money. This is because different countries use different coins. Part of the fun of going abroad, usually on holiday or for a school trip, is having different coins in your pocket. The more you travel, the more you realize just how boring the money is in this country. Yes! Foreign money is much more fun. Until you try to spend it! The first big problem is working out how much everything costs. Oh yes, you've been told that 234 Dublonkies is worth 57p, but do you really want to be doing a major mathematical calculation every time you want to buy a bag of crisps?

ARE YOU SURE THIS IS RIGHT? I COULD BUY A SMALL HOUSE WITH THIS LOT BACK HOME!

The other problem is that – if you're on a school trip – you want your mates to think that you're well travelled and have a reasonable command of the local currency. And that's the biggest problem.

How to cope
You can of course try always paying with a bank note. The problems with this are:

a) you might be handing over a thousand-pound note for something that costs 20p. And...

b) you're almost certainly going to wind up with a mountain of small coins, so much so that you won't be able to walk.

So how do you cope? Go into the shop with confidence, pick up the thing you want to buy and take it to the counter. Remember you are not trying to impress the shop owner. This is impossible anyway, because she already knows that you're a tourist; the naff tourist baseball cap is a bit of a give away,[1] not to mention your total lack of command of the local language. But you do want to impress your mates/family. So you pull out a handful of coins and start pretending to count them out with the speed and accuracy of a native. As you do this, drop a couple and then say: "These coins are so fiddly! Here – help yourself!" So saying, you toss the handful of coins on to the counter. If you can accompany this action with

1: Give away? You're joking! It cost £15! Or rather 2000.7 Dublonkies.

a bit of jibberish, your mates will probably think you're talking the local language even though the shopkeeper won't. The shopkeeper will help themselves to the right money, you'll scoop up the change and everything will be fine. As long as the shopkeeper is honest. If they aren't then you really might end up paying £2,000 for a bag of crisps!

NOTE: you can buy currency converters that sort out the exchange rate for you. The only thing is that if you're clever enough to work one of those you're clever enough to do it in your head!

Finders Keepers

What is it?
It's an expression that means if you find something you should be allowed to keep it. Of course, sometimes the thing you find isn't actually lost. A horse wandering along the road, for instance, might not actually be lost; it might just have seen a gate open and gone for a walk. Besides, would you really want to keep a huge great horse, especially when cleaning out the mouse cage is such a pain every week? Of course, money is different. A ten pence piece lying around on the floor is very inviting. You pick it up, call out "Finders Keepers!" and as far as you're concerned you are 10p better off and that's an end to it.

Unfortunately, it's usually only just the beginning.

"Have you found some money?" asks dad.

"Yes," you innocently reply.

"Well, if it's got the Queen's head on it, it's mine."

"No it's not! It's my 20p piece!" pipes up Little Brother.

"It's only 10p," you point out. "So it can't be yours!"

"Yes! That's half of it!"

And so begins the worst family feud since Auntie Mable died and left her teeth in her will.

Anyway, back to the 10p. Mum has now joined the queue of claimants. Your elder sister has brought along a lawyer who is trying to explain the laws of treasure trove, which up until now have never actually been applied to a dropped 10p. Your chances of hanging on to your new-found "fortune" are quickly slipping away.

How to cope

If you see a coin, do the following in this order:

1. Pick it up.
2. Shut up about it.

If somebody has lost it and they ask you about it, you can always say: "Yes, I've got it. I put it in my pocket for safekeeping." If you start asking around to try and find the owner, you'll discover that everyone within a 30-mile radius will have lost it. Of course, if you find a wallet stuffed with credit cards and cash and stuff, you should take it straight to the nearest police station. If you ask around, again you'll discover that amazingly everyone has just lost their wallet.

Forgery

What is it?

Since money was first used there have always been unscrupulous people who have tried to forge it. In the early days this was very easy. After all, one shell looked more or less the same as another, as did one feather or one lump of bronze. Who was to say which one was actually money and which one wasn't? This is why lumps of bronze were stamped, so that everyone knew that they were really coins. These days coins and banknotes are very sophisticated, even if the English banknotes *do* all look the same.

HOW CAN YOU TELL THIS £12 NOTE IS A FORGERY?

The paper that banknotes are printed on carries a water mark, although why anyone would imagine that dribbling a bit of water on a banknote would stop somebody forging it beats me. Ha! Ha! Actually, a water mark is something inside the paper that can only be seen by holding it up to the light. Banknotes also carry a very fine strip of metal through them which also makes them very hard to forge. But people still do it, sometimes very successfully. So much so that many shops, pubs, restaurants and even taxis now carry a little detection machine. It's a light that they hold the note under and it tells them that it's a forgery. You can also get an anti-forgery pen. So as you can see – forgery doesn't really pay.

How to cope

Since you're unlikely to take up forgery, beyond the odd note to get you off games, there's really nothing to cope with. Although if you are caught with a forged note it's another matter. The shop keeper treats you as though you actually forged the note yourself. They say things like:

"Did you know that this tenner is a forgery?"

Surely that has to be the stupidest question, ever? If you did know then presumably you were trying to pass it off as real, in which case you're hardly likely to admit it, are you? And if you didn't know, are they ever going to believe you? Maybe the only way of coping is to carry your own anti-forgery kit.

By the way, during the Second World War the Nazis forged millions of English pound notes. The idea was to drop them by plane, all over Britain. People would then pick them up and try to spend them. Money was so short during the war, apparently, that nobody was really bothered where it came from, even if it did fall out of the sky. Because forgery was (and is) illegal, German High Command believed that the English would be so busy arresting people for forgery that they wouldn't have time to fight the war.[1]

WOULD YOU BELIEVE IT, A SUITCASE FULL OF MONEY JUST APPEARED FROM NOWHERE!

DONK!

In the event, very few notes were actually dropped. I suppose that the pilots thought "stuff this for a game of soldiers" and flew to the Bahamas, where they lived the millionaire lifestyle, forging friendships with forged money.

Funds

What are they?
The term "funds" can mean several things. It can mean money, as in the bank manager writing to tell you that you have insufficient funds in your account.[2] It can also mean something that has been set up to raise money for

---

1: This isn't strictly true. Actually they believed that people would realize that the notes were forgeries and stop trusting the government, and therefore stop fighting for them. Which I personally think is even more far fetched than my explanation, even if it is true!
2: Which is bank-speak for broke.

something, such as the *Save the Lifeboat Fund*. Or the *Rebuild the Church Spire Fund*. Or the *Feed the Rabbit Fund*. Yes! I think I've just hit on a great money-making scheme. After all, one of the greatest expenses is feeding your pet, isn't it? All that hard-earned pocket money going into the bottomless pit known as Bunnikins. But if you were to set up a fund to help feed him that would take the pressure off your already over-stretched purse strings.

There are of course snags, as you might imagine. People are going to be unlikely to give you money to feed your rabbit. After all, they've probably got rabbits of their own.

How to cope
Well, of course, you can't really. Forget I ever mentioned it. A rabbit feeding fund is a silly idea – unless *you* can make it work!

Gift token

What is it?
This is rather like a book token but isn't restricted to books, so as a form of money it's usually a lot more flexible. I say usually because it's relatives who generally give you these gift tokens, and because of that the

tokens they buy you tend only to be redeemable (cashable) at really obscure stores, like *Horrocks Edible Underwear*. Oh yes, just the sort of thing you want to sink you fortune into, I don't think.

How to cope

A relative can usually be found who is more gullible than you are. Maybe not much more but frankly the degree of gullible-ness is not important; off-loading the token is. Of course, because the token is a bit obscure (a *bit*!), you may have to negotiate the price: a £10 token for edible underwear might be worth, say, £7. The trick is to get the best price you can and shake on the deal before little brother/sister changes their mind!

Going "Dutch"

What is it?

Well for a start it's not putting on wooden shoes and talking about tulips; it means sharing the cost of something.

This is great if you're on a date and you know that it's likely to cost you more than you've actually got. Nothing jumps into the path of true love and pulls a totally scary face faster than lack of cash. But the going Dutch-ness of the date has to be established before the date starts. It's no good taking your date to a posh restaurant,[1] then saying as the bill arrives: "Your half comes to £4.75." This is not on the Top Ten List of Great Ways to Impress Your Date. Neither is saying: "You pay the bill while I go to the loo and I'll settle up with you later."

How to cope

As you might imagine, going Dutch is a tricky business. One way to establish it is to be totally honest, and say: "I'd really like to go to the movies with you, but I'm a bit short of cash. How about going Dutch?" That instantly gets rid of anyone who's after your fortune. Unfortunately, there's an unwritten law of Human Nature that says that the ones that fancy you for all the wrong reasons are the ones you fancy the most.

If you don't feel brave enough to go for the direct approach, then plan B is probably your best option: make sure you've got enough cash on you to pay for the evening just in case things go terribly wrong. Beg off

1: OK – McDonald's.

your brothers and sisters if you really must, but don't make the fatal mistake of going into details about why you need the cash. They will taunt you for ever if you do! Once fully armed with plenty of dosh, meet your date and proceed to the cinema.

At the box office check the price of the tickets and then fumble in your pockets. *Don't say*: "Can my friend get in for half price as he/she's not very tall?" That would not be wise; it would be silly in fact. Of course, if you want to go for *TOTALLY STUPID*, you could say: "If we start snogging and miss a bit of the film, can we have a partial refund?" That will guarantee that the evening won't cost you a penny, because your date will disappear as fast as light or even faster. It's better not to say anything. Also, you mustn't look as though you're desperately searching for cash. It's better that everyone thinks that you're so used to carrying great wads of the stuff that your pockets are the size of a small South American country. During this "performance" your date may do one of a number of things:

1. Say: "Here, let me get the tickets." To which you *do not* reply "I was hoping you'd say that" even if you're thinking it. Try saying something like: "That's very kind of you to offer. We could go halves if you like."
2. Your date may just stand there and watch you. In which case you have to pull your money out, pay up and look forward to several months working as your sibling's personal slave.

Of course, the more dare-devil among you might want to opt for the following ploy: Make a forged £50 note. They're pink, I think. I once heard someone talk about one and I think they said that they were pink. Wave this at the cinema cashier and say: "Sorry, I haven't got anything smaller." The cashier will refuse to change it, partly because she'll assume that it's a forgery (and she'd be right) and partly because she won't believe that it's your money (and she'd be right again – it isn't *anybody*'s money! It isn't even *money*!) Your date, assuming that you're loaded, will offer to pay for the tickets. Once inside the cinema you go to the loo and "lose" your £50 note. You come back to your seat and explain, saying something like: "I've just been robbed in the loo by a daring gang of international £50 note thieves, who deftly made their escape through a tiny skylight to a waiting helicopter. We could chase after them on our bikes, but they'll probably be miles away by now."

Try and be subtle about it, obviously. You then produce your *actual* money and say: "I've still got £5.37. So I'll be able to treat us to something to eat later."

"We'll go halves," pipes up your date, almost as though they've been programmed. Sorted.

All right – one ploy. And not a very good one at that. Sorry.

"Going rate", The

What is it?

The going rate is an expression that refers to the cost or value of something. For instance, the going rate for cleaning a car might be £5. It *might* be, but you're never likely to get it![1] The going rate is important when you're negotiating a price for any jobs your parents want you to do. Yes, I know I said earlier that you should try to avoid getting hooked into doing regular jobs because that makes it very difficult to renegotiate a pay rise. But sometimes it's unavoidable, especially if you've got brothers or sisters who are just waiting to take the job off you. This also makes the going rate very hard to negotiate, because whatever price you suggest they'll be prepared to do it cheaper.

How to cope

The first thing to establish is that you're the best person for the job; as in business the cheapest is not necessarily the best. Take car cleaning for example: you need to

---

1: If your parents will pay £5 for cleaning cars, drop me a line and I'll pop round and clean it. Although I might have to charge travel expenses on top so it could work out expensive (with any luck!).

convince the parent involved that they not only want their car clean but that they want it to *stay* clean, at least until it gets dirty again. Yes – I know that doesn't make sense, but don't worry, adults never notice things like that. They'll probably be prepared to pay a bit more for the reassurance that the job will be well done.[1] Having established a fair price,[2] then clean the car brilliantly well, inside and out. Depending on your bribery skills you may be able to get somebody else to do this for you. Then invite said parent to examine your handiwork. It helps at this point if you can arrange for a few passers-by to … er … pass by and admire your efforts. You can probably pick up a few willing old people at the local day-care centre. After all, they like to feel useful and they don't get out much. Get them to walk by and say something like: "New car, Mr Philips?" or whatever your parent's name is.

A few words of warning here:

a) Don't get them all to pass by together and chorus their comments; a small group of shuffling old lunatics all speaking together just might give the game away.

1: Although don't hold your breath!
2: i.e. ridiculously high.

b) Make sure that they don't actually say: "New car, Mr Philips?" unless it's your dad they're talking to and that's his name. Again this can be a bit of a giveaway.

Having established that you are far and away the best car cleaner in the neighbourhood (if not exactly the cheapest) you set about making the job pay. The first thing you need to do is to make sure that the payment is secure whatever happens. This should be fairly easy, as it's just a question of establishing that you'll clean the car on a given day and get a fixed rate for doing it, with no strings attached. Having got this sorted, the next stage in the operation is to reduce the amount of time you have to spend cleaning the car. Carefully study the weather reports and try and arrange to clean the car just as a storm is breaking out. Your parent will insist that you abandon the cleaning for fear of you dying of pneumonia, and they'll still pay you as long as you point out that you would have finished the cleaning but for the fact that they stopped you. Always try and put the blame for the job not being completed on your parent; never be the one to suggest that you should stop. Once you've got this regular job firmly established you may even be able to persuade your little brother to clean the car for you – for a fraction of the money that you get paid.

This is called sub-contracting, which basically means that you get somebody else to do it and you pocket most of the dosh. This is always a good idea because if Little Brother makes a pig's ear of the job – which he almost certainly will – you can blame him, which means that he's never likely to be in a position to steal the job away from you.

Holiday money

What is it?
We talked about this at length earlier, but what I never did was explain any strategies for avoiding the holiday money problems that I'd outlined. So I'll do it now.

How to cope
The trickiest thing about holidays is hanging on to your cash and spending it on having the kind of good time that you promised yourself whilst you were struggling to scrape the money together. But this strategy will help:

A few days before the holiday starts, work yourself into a state of panic. Watching *Home and Away* should help – it's full of teenagers in a state of panic so you should easily be able to find a role model.

TOO LITTLE | TOO MUCH | JUST RIGHT

Having achieved the right level of distraught child, head off to your parent and tell them, as tearfully as possible, that your carefully gathered holiday money has disappeared. There's no real need to go into details. You don't, for example, need to invent a tale about standing there helpless while it spontaneously combusted. The mere fact that you are beside yourself with grief will be enough to persuade your parent that you have a problem. They won't want you to grieve too long, as they can't really handle emotions.[1] "Don't worry about it," they'll say. "We'll make sure you have spending money on holiday."

This is actually the last thing you want, but don't worry, I'll show you the way round it. If your parents insist on paying, since you've got no money, you just opt for the most expensive of everything. You'll soon have them refusing to bankroll you. Your siblings will come in handy at this point, because they can always be relied upon to point out that it isn't fair that your parents are paying for you when they are having to use their own money. Pretty soon your family will be happy to leave you back at the hotel struggling to complete the hotel's only jigsaw which has most of the bits missing, or playing *Scrabble* with the landlady's deaf and dyslexic granny.

I DON'T THINK "FLANDYCOSS" IS A REAL WORD

WHAT'S THAT, A TRIPLE WORD SCORE? OH, GOODIE!

1: Their own or other people's.

Once the family have gone off to do family things, you can take yourself and your cash off out for a day of real excitement. A couple of words of warning though: always make sure that you know roughly what time your family will be returning to the hotel, and *never* boast to your brothers and sisters about the fabulous time you're having, because they'll almost certainly shop you to mum and dad. Or even worse than that, they'll insist on coming with you!

I.O.U.

What is it?

When people borrow money from each other they sometimes sign a slip of paper saying: "I.O.U. (or I Owe You) the sum of X amount, signed...", and if you're lucky they'll actually sign it! You've probably opened up your money box and found a scrap of paper in there saying "I.O.U. £5" at which point you instantly know that one of your parents has been raiding your money box again. Unfortunately, most parents "forget" to sign the note, and so it isn't always easy to work out who's "borrowed" it. Getting it back is even harder!

This is a difficult one because unless you know which parent has helped themselves and left the I.O.U., it's quite tricky to insist that they repay you. Logic might tell you that the fact that they've left an I.O.U. in the first place is proof of their intention to repay the money. But you're old enough to have realized that "logic" and parents" don't mix.

How to cope

As you will know, I don't usually suggest persuading your brother or sister to help you, mainly because I know from experience that this rarely works. But in some situations it's the only solution; and this is just such a situation. Tell your brother/sister that your cash would be a lot safer if you stored it in each other's money boxes. Obviously, get them to swear on pain of death or something even worse that they will never touch your money (or even sniff it for that matter). Having made this pact your money will now be safely in their money box in their bedroom, whilst their money will be in your money box in your bedroom. With me so far? Good! At this point it might help things if you boast openly, in front of your parents, about the vast amount of money you've managed to save. This ensures that if they go searching for emergency milk money, they are far more likely to dip into the money box in your room than in anyone else's. Thus whenever they "borrow" money they'll actually be borrowing your brother/sister's money, not yours!

Obviously you'll need to back your sibling up (ever so slightly) when they attempt to get the "borrowed" money back, but only because you may need them in the (unlikely) event of it ever happening to you.

Jobs

What are they?

You'll be pleased to hear that they've made shoving 8-year-olds up chimneys illegal,[1] but at 13 you can get a paper round. Paper rounds were always traditionally the way teenagers first start to scrape a decent amount of money together. Billions of bikes have been paid for with paper rounds. I think I got my first "proper" bike by doing a paper round. By "proper" I mean with loads of gears and accessories. I also worked for the milkman, delivering milk – not surprisingly. The great thing about this sort of job is that it brings in more cash than running errands for mum and dad. You are also definitely going to get paid, whereas mum and dad will do everything that they possibly can to wriggle out of paying you. But paper shops and milk companies *have* to pay you, or they get into trouble. Unfortunately, all these jobs involve getting up very early and going out in all weathers.

THERE HAS GOT TO BE AN EASIER WAY TO MAKE A LIVING!

1: Unless of course you have an 8-year-old sibling.

They aren't something you can do only when you feel like it. People need their milk and their papers, usually before they go to work. My milkman delivers at four o'clock in the morning! Mind you, he is a bit mad.

How to cope
Obviously getting up really, really early and tramping round the streets delivering newspapers or milk is not everybody's idea of fun, even if it does bring in extra money. So the problem is how to earn a paper deliverer's wages without putting yourself through too much extremely dangerous exercise. Hmmm … it's a tricky one. I may need to go and make a cup of tea and think about it. Won't be a minute. Maybe you'd like to read on while I do that.

Kiss-o-grams

What are they?
Anyone who's ever been to their elder brother/sister's birthday party (even if they were there in disguise) will know that one of the worst things about getting older is that so-called friends spring surprises on you. And one of the popular surprises at the moment is a Kiss-o-gram. A total stranger turns up on your doorstep dressed as Tarzan, Tinky Winky or Elvis Presley.[1]

1: Actually if somebody turns up on your doorstep dressed as Elvis, it probably really is Elvis. He isn't dead, you know! Ask anybody!

The person who opened the door lets them in, for some strange reason, and they proceed to kiss the person who's birthday it is. This sort of thing also happens at weddings, anniversaries and funerals, although it's usually less successful at funerals; I can't imagine why. Kiss-o-grams are hideous in every way and deeply embarrassing.

How to cope

Just avoid them. But why am I telling you about Kiss-o-grams in a book about cash? Well, it suddenly occurred to me that they were a good way of making money.

Now, before you start shouting: "No way! I'm not charging round the streets in fancy dress in all weathers! I'd rather have a paper round!"[2], I wasn't seriously suggesting that you did that. I was thinking more about a sort of Non-kiss-o-gram, which entails you threatening to kiss people unless they give you money. A word of warning: don't try this on your Auntie Doreen, the one with the beard; she'll kiss anyone. Believe me – I *know*!

2: I still haven't solved the paper round problem by the way. But I will! Maybe.

Loans

What are they?

In simple terms, they are sums of money that you borrow from somebody. Somebody like a relative. Unfortunately, borrowing from anyone who knows you can be terribly complicated. Just try borrowing some cash from your sister/brother and see what happens!

How to cope

Don't do it! You already know that if you lend somebody money it gives you the upper hand. I've already explained elsewhere in the book that having your parent(s) owe you money can be a useful tool in your struggle to get your own way. But if the situation were reversed … point taken?

Money box

What is it?
It's a box that you keep your money in. It might be cunningly disguised as *My Little Pony* with a large slot between its buttocks where you poke in your pocket money, or something in less good taste, but it's still just a box where you keep your money. And as such, it can easily find itself prey to parents with poor housekeeping skills, or siblings with light fingers.

How to cope
Keep it locked. Double locked. Triple locked. And hire a guard dog. Maybe even a private security firm.

Notes

What are they?
I'm not referring to the little notes that your parents leave in your money box, notes that say things like: "Borrowed a fiver to pay the milkman."

This entry is really about banknotes, or paper money as they are sometimes called. Nice, aren't they? Especially when they are new. There's nothing better than opening a birthday card and watching a brand new, crisp £10 note flutter out. A word of warning here: if you think a birthday card is likely to contain a banknote, don't open it anywhere near the dog; dogs are so stupid that they are likely to think that it's some new form of flying food and eat it. Have you any idea how much a vet charges to cut your dog open to get a tenner back? Lots!

Anyway, having got your brand-new, crisp £10 note, you start to fantasize about ways of spending it. You make a list of all the things you want; by the time the list has covered two sides of one page in an exercise book, you realize that £10 really isn't a lot of money. But it's all you've got so you fold it carefully and place it safely in your pocket before setting off to town for a shopping "spree". You've been extra-cautious; you've managed to avoid telling your mum or dad that you're going shopping so that there's no chance of them coming with you and offering to spend your money for you on something sensible. So what can possibly go wrong?

Well, I don't know whether you've noticed this but banknotes have a nasty habit of disguising themselves as bits of scrap paper. It's basically a design fault that has never been cured. It doesn't matter how carefully or neatly you fold the note and place it in your pocket, within minutes it will look like that old chocolate bar wrapper that you keep meaning to throw away. And you can bet all the money[1] you like that the moment you decide to bin that wrapper is the moment that it isn't a wrapper at all, but your precious £10's worth of birthday money.

How to cope

Thankfully, the Bank of England are trying to solve the problem for you. Banknotes are slowly being replaced by coins. As I write, a £5 coin has been issued. By the time you read this there may well be a £10 coin, even a £20 one. The only worrying thing about this is the fact that each coin is bigger than the last.

Whilst the cheaper coins are getting so small that you can hardly see them, the dearer coins are getting larger. The £2 coin is about twice the size of the £1 coin, and the £5 one is even bigger again. My concern is that there will eventually be coins that are too big to carry in your pocket. Worse still – too big to hide from light-fingered parents! But in the meantime, how are you going to cope with that tenner? Get a wallet; or a purse; preferably one with a huge combination padlock on. I say a combination lock because many parents are quite nifty at picking locks! Then place your neatly folded £10 note

1: Although, of course, you can't bet any money *at all* if you've just mistakenly thrown it away.

into the wallet/purse and lock it. That way, when you arrive at the shop of your choice you can unlock your wallet and go: "Hang on! How did that screwed-up, old chocolate bar wrapper get in there? And where's my tenner?"

Old money

What is it?
You've probably heard your granny or your Great-uncle Bill saying:

WHAT'S THIS IN OLD MONEY?

WHAT'S "OLD MONEY"?

What they are talking about is money before decimalization, which happened in 1971. Before that, English money was in pounds, shillings and pence, measurements were in feet and inches, and Margate was still in Kent; so you see not everything has changed. Before decimalization things were very confusing. For instance, there were 12 inches to the foot, 3 feet to the yard and 1,760 yards to the mile. In fact there still are, and it's still confusing. But while much of the rest of the world had a system based on the number ten, we pressed on with our very confusing system. Until 1971, when it was decided that we should make things much easier for ourselves by using the same system as everybody else. But the change to decimalization itself caused a massive amount of confusion, especially for old people, some of whom found zebra crossings confusing, mainly because there were never any zebras on them. A quick look at the chart below, which compares old and new money, might help explain why old people (and some younger people!) were so confused:

OLD	NEW EQUIVALENT
Penny	ONE TWELFTH OF 5p
12 Pennies = 1 shilling	5p
2 shillings	10p
2 shillings & 6 pence = half a crown	$12\frac{1}{2}$ p
10 shillings	50p
20 shillings	1 POUND

As you can see, the old system was very confusing.

How to cope

You don't have to! The present system works fine. You just have to hope that they don't change it again!

Owing money

See DEBT

Pet costs

What is it?

Pets are lovely, aren't they? Especially rabbits. I love rabbits, although I couldn't eat a whole one. Only joking! But one thing that pets do (apart from smell) is cost money. OK, so you might not have to cough up to own one – parents have a knack of buying you a gerbil when you've asked for a bike – but in the long run you'll be made to pay.

"Well, it's quite like a bike," says mum/dad/annoying relative as they hand over the present. "You still have to clean it every week." Yes, but you can't ride a gerbil, unless you've got extremely short legs. And you don't have to feed a bike.[1]

Gerbils are another matter. You now find yourself the proud owner of the only gerbil that does nothing but eat. And eat and eat. It has no hobbies. It won't play in its wheel or with any of its toys. Not that it's actually got a wheel or toys. Well, you can't afford any extras once you've paid out for food every week. And then there's the natural consequence of overeating.

You know what I'm talking about. Arthur (as you've named your gerbil for some strange reason) needs cleaning out every day. And bedding isn't cheap. By the time you've finished paying out just to keep your pet *alive*, you've got through all your pocket money, odd-job money, Little Brother Protection Money and anything else that comes your way via bribery (nasty), blackmail (even worse) or any other foul but worthwhile money-making scheme.

1: You don't even have to clean it if you've got a smaller brother/sister who has a guilty secret, but that's another matter!

How to cope

This is a tricky one because pets have feelings too; hard to believe I know, but it's true apparently. Therefore, your lack of money shouldn't really reflect on them. Why should they starve just because your parents are too mean to give you enough pocket money? However, the simple fact of the matter is that you just don't have enough dosh to feed and care for your pet as well as buying your own essentials, such as sweets and mags, and saving up for the latest computer game, *Mindless Violence with a Ridiculous-Looking Gun IV*.

Which is where your parents come in. Encourage your parent(s) to be involved in the development of your pet. OK, so most pets just sit there looking bored, but your parent(s) can get involved in that as well.

Perhaps you could even get books out of the library on your chosen pet. *The Gerbil – A Friend for Life*; that would be a good one to get. *101 Things To Do with a Dead Rodent* wouldn't. Toss casual "interesting" facts about your pet into the conversation.[1] *DO NOT AT ANY POINT* ever say: "I wanted a bike but you bought me this useless gerbil" even if you're thinking it; even if the gerbil's thinking it too.

1: This is also a handy way of changing the subject if you think that your parent is about to tell you off.

If you don't overdo this, your parent should soon develop a keen interest in your pet. Telltale signs that your scheme is working will be comments from them along the lines of: "I see Arthur has been to the loo this morning."1 Comments like this mean that your parent is hooked, well and truly. It shouldn't take long; after all, parents are simple-minded creatures who don't get out much, so the toilet habits of your pet will be totally awe-inspiring for them. Once you're sure that your parent has the best interests of your pet at heart, you can start saying things like: "Arthur's really wonderful, but I would like to do more for him, like feed him regularly. But I'm on a really tight budget." Then wait for the magic words:

"Well, maybe I could help out."

"How?" you ask, all wide-eyed and innocent.

"Well, perhaps I could chip in with the occasional bag of food or bail of straw."

Then you move in for the kill, getting the whole thing on a proper (regular) footing:

"How occasional? What about every Thursday?"

And then I think you'll find that everything is – as they say – *sorted*!

1: Of course, it might not actually have been this morning. It might not in fact have been this *week* – it rather depends on how often you clean the thing out!

Phone bill

What is it?

Unless I've been totally misinformed, it's the bill you pay for having a phone. But it is also the cause of more rows in most households than anything else, including superglueing your sister to the ceiling.[1]

The problem is the fact that the bills can be itemized which means that every call made is listed. This is probably the least child-friendly invention ever thought of, if you don't count school, homework, tidying your room and washing. What makes it even worse is that parents love to study the phone bill.

1: This is not a good idea. She is almost certainly going to come unstuck just as you are having your breakfast, and a large sister floating about in your cornflakes is not something you need first thing in the morning.

They can't just *pay* it. This is because they lead very dreary lives and hardly anyone can be bothered to write to them, except to ask for money. None of which explains why they should blame *you*, just because the phone bill is three times as expensive as normal. What do they expect you to do – never contact your friends? If you did that, they'd start worrying that you had *no* friends. Even their argument that you could have said whatever you wanted to say to your friends whilst you were at school doesn't make sense either. If you did that you'd get told off for talking in class – or even *shouting* in class if your friend goes to a different school. No – the logical way to discuss all the really important stuff of life with your friends is by phone. But do you think that your parents understand that kind of argument? Of course they don't.

How to cope

This is quite a tricky one because parents are very blinkered where *their* money is concerned. If you do run up a large phone bill they're likely to ban you from phoning your friends. So the thing to do is to find out the phone number of somebody who lives near to your best friend; somebody you know, but not too well. We'll call this person Mrs Johnson. You then tell your parents that you need to phone a friend about your homework.

"No way, José!" will be the reply, even if your name's Colin.

"Well, can I phone Mrs Johnson, then? She lives over the road from Sharon? She could pop round and ask Sharon to phone me?"[1]

They will agree to let you call her; reluctantly, but they will agree. You check that your parents aren't listening and then you phone Mrs Johnson and chat for as long as possible. This will be extremely difficult as you'll run out of things to say just after you say: "Is that you, Mrs Johnson?" But just keep going; talk rubbish; repeat yourself; talk rubbish; repeat yourself; she'll never notice. She'll just be so pleased that somebody wants to chat to her, even though you actually don't. After a (long) while you say: "I've forgotten what I called you about now, but it's not important anyway. Bye." And ring off. Are you with me so far? Good, because this is complex, but worth it.

Now, when the monthly statement comes through your parents will go bananas. Roll with it. Don't worry; it's going to be OK, I promise.

"What the heck is this? £50 for a call to Mrs Johnson?"
You then say:
"Yes. Sorry about that, but I couldn't shut her up."[2]
If they check with her, she's bound to say: "Oh yes!

1: What do you mean "Who's Sharon?". She's your best friend.
2: Sorry, Mrs Johnson!

113

We had a lovely long chat." and your parents will assume that it was Mrs Johnson who kept the conversation going, because they know she's a bit of a gossip.[1] Your parents will then ban you from ever phoning her again, agreeing – *and this is the important bit* – to let you phone your friends, just as long as you keep the call shorter than the one you had with Mrs Johnson. Which means that, as long as you can keep Mrs Johnson chatting for – say – an hour in the first place, you'll have got yourself just under an hour's talk time to chat to your mates – without any hassle! Possibly; although I wouldn't bank on it. After all, you know how devious parents can be!

Pocket money

What is it?
This is something that causes almost as much trouble in the average household as the argument about who's turn it is to forget to feed the animals. Logic tells you that you should be getting as much pocket money as your mates. After all, that's what they get; as much as *their* mates. All their mates except you, anyway.

Unfortunately, this kind of logic is lost on your average parent, who probably doesn't see why you *need* pocket money anyway; after all, you'll only spend it.

I'VE JUST BOUGHT YOU THIS SUPER JUMPER, SO YOU WON'T NEED POCKET MONEY THIS WEEK TO BUY CLOTHES

HOW ABOUT POCKET MONEY TO EMIGRATE?

1: Sorry again, Mrs Johnson!

And this is where they miss the point: that's what pocket money is for – spending. It isn't money that is attached to some specific job; at least it *shouldn't* be. And this is also another mistake that parents make. They firmly believe that pocket money is something they give you in return for jobs that you do for them. No! Sorry, parents! That's just not on! Pocket money is pocket money; it's money that goes in your pocket for you to do with, as you will. You're free to save it, spend it, give it away to a worthy cause; even give it back to your parents if you really want to![1]

Of course, parents don't understand this. Some don't even see why *they* should be giving you pocket money in the first place.

How to cope
The first thing you have to do is clearly establish that your parents understand the meaning of pocket money. They need to realize that it's all part of growing up. Learning to handle money is an essential step along the rocky road to adulthood.

IF I NEVER LEARN HOW TO HANDLE MONEY, I COULD GROW UP LIKE DAD!

CARS

Some parents may try and get around this by letting you play with their money for 20 minutes at the weekend, but you have to make them realize that this is not the

1: If you find yourself wanting to do this, lie down for a bit; the feeling will pass. If it doesn't, go and see a doctor – it's not normal!

same thing at all. The money has to be yours and yours alone. Yours alone – not yours, a loan; this has to be money they've given you to keep.

Having established that and having got your hands on even a small amount of money, the big problem is going to be getting your parent to leave you to look after the money all on your own. This is part of letting go and something that many parents find very hard. After all, they probably earned that money, they may even have had it for a long time, they've become attached to it; it's almost part of the family. Watching it go off to McDonald's without knowing whether they'll ever see it again can be deeply stressful. So you need to reassure them that you'll look after the money, see it safely across the road and so on, and never let it out of your sight, at least until you spend it.

It's a good idea if the first few times you get pocket money that you buy something you can take back to show your parents. If you're really brave you might even let them watch you spend it, although as I've said many times in this book they'll only try and put you off. But if you can bear this, it is at least one way of letting your parents see that the money isn't gone, it's just turned into something else; transfigured, if you like.

After a while, if all goes according to plan, your parents will stop worrying about what time your pocket money comes home, until eventually they won't care whether it comes home or not. You, of course, will always be a different matter. Whatever time you come home, they'll still want to know why you're so late. That is one battle you'll never win, I'm afraid!

Queen, The

What is it? Sorry – what is she?
Why should the Queen be in a book about cash? Well, apart from the fact that she is one of the richest people on the planet (if not the galaxy[1]), she never carries any cash, apparently. I wonder if these facts are in any way linked? After all, if you never carried any dosh you wouldn't be able to spend any, would you? The rest of the royal family don't carry any money either. One thing Prince Charles has probably never said is: "I think I've lost a 20p piece. If you find it, it's got a picture of Mummy on it."

So how do they pay for things? The simple answer is that they probably don't. After all, if you ran a shop and the Queen came in and said: "Copy of the *Sun* please," are you going to insist that she pays? Of course not.

1: Not the galaxy, actually. The average *little green man in the street* on the Planet BnxaURTa is a trillionaire.

You're far more likely to say: "There you go, Ma'am. It's on me." All the shops around the royal residences must lose a fortune in profit, especially if the royals are nipping in every few minutes for milk, dog biscuits and all those other little things that they're likely to forget when they go to the supermarket. But what about if the shop keeper doesn't believe in royalty? What about if they would like England to have a president like Bill Clinton, or maybe Baby Spice? In which case, I think it's very unlikely that they are going to say to Her Majesty: "There you go, luv – those *were* King Edward's potatoes, but they're yours now."

How to cope, Your Majesty

Assuming that Her Majesty is not reading this book,[1] I will let you into a royal secret. If the Queen, or any other royal, finds themselves a bit short of the ready folding stuff – which she will every day if she doesn't carry any – she simply turns to her personal detective and says: "Pay the commoner."

And her policeman gets his wallet out; and it's a big one. Yes! That bulge in his jacket pocket is not a Smith and Weston or a hand-crafted set of Ninja throwing stars, it's

1: If you are Your Majesty, then welcome to my book. I suppose that a knighthood's out of the question?

118

actually a wallet stuffed with dosh, all of which, ironically, has got the Queen's head on it. But where does all this cash come from? Surely it can't belong to the policeman himself because the police are very badly paid. In fact, they earn less than teachers without the benefit of all those massively long holidays; and they have to work at weekends and hang around with naughty people. So, I think if they had to dish the dosh for the royal family on top of all that it would be so unfair. But you'll be pleased to hear that they don't use their own cash. No, the cash they use comes out of something called the Royal Purse, which I assume is a purse where the Royal Family keep their wonga. It must be pretty big is all I can say. After all, the amount the Queen must have to shell out on dog biscuits alone would probably feed a small country for a month or more. I've just thought: does the Queen have any say in what she looks like on the coins and banknotes? Can she tell them to change the lot if, for instance, they make her nose look a bit big, or her teeth look like they've got a bit of cabbage stuck between them?

And who decides which crown she wears on which coin, because – checking my money – I notice she looks different on each one. Well, not that different, but I've noticed that she's wearing a much bigger crown on the pound coin from the one she wears on the penny. Maybe it's a case of the higher the value of the coin, the bigger the crown; so if they introduce a £10 coin she'll probably look like she's got a large teapot on her head.

It must be tough being royalty. Do you think that Prince William will break with tradition and start carrying money when he becomes King? He'd be a fool if he did. After all, why put your hand in your *own* pocket when you can get your personal policeman to pay for everything?

Relatives

What are they?
In the unlikely event of you being a member of the Royal Family, you are going to have to look for other ways to avoid parting with your hard-earned cash, or making more. This can be where relatives come in. Yes, they're not just there to humiliate you by trying to kiss you, ruffle your hair or knit you horrible jumpers; they can be a useful source of extra cash. But they have to be approached with caution. In my experience, aunts and uncles are usually good for a pound or two. This is largely due to the fact that they are your parents' brothers and/or sisters, and so there's a certain amount

of rivalry about trying to appear more generous than your parents are. They needn't worry: *everybody* appears more generous than parents without making any effort at all. Grannies and granddads are also a handy source of extra dosh, except that most of them haven't quite caught up with inflation,[1] and so they still think that there are things that exist that only cost 5p, or a shilling as some of them still call the 5p coin.[2]

The biggest problem with relatives is that many of them don't visit that often and so you have to make the most of this rare money-raising opportunity.

How to cope
There are various strategies that you can employ in order to capitalize on a visit from a relative.

Because there's probably a certain element of relatives trying to outdo your parents, it's a good idea to try and plant the idea into the visiting relatives' minds that your mum or dad have just been very generous to you. Aunts and uncles usually get taken in by this fairly easily. But how do you do it? Remember that timing is everything.

1: Inflation is the rate at which prices rise and fall. Well, rise anyway!
2: See also OLD MONEY

It may be that your uncle (or aunt) always presses a pound coin into your hand as they leave, in which case you've probably got plenty of time to work on them. You can do this by getting out an expensive-looking toy and playing with it under their nose; or in the case of a CD, tape, video or computer game, you start playing it loudly. This could be something you had as a birthday or Christmas present, or even something you've borrowed from a friend just for the occasion. Once you've got their attention they will say something like:

You could also throw in a quick "It cost a fortune" for good measure, but it's best not to overdo it.

A few words of warning here:

1. Make sure it *is* actually expensive (£10 or more).
2. Make sure that it isn't something that they bought you.[1] This may seem obvious, but you'd be amazed how often you can get caught out in this way.
3. Oh – and don't do this in front of your parents, especially if they actually *haven't* played any part in you obtaining the particular item. Parents are notorious for saying: "No, I didn't!" and blowing your scam. This is amazing because in most other ways parents are incredibly good at taking the credit for things that they've played no part in – such as your upbringing, education, etc.

1: See also THANK YOU LETTERS

Having established the (supposed) generosity of your parents, leave your relative to ponder this. Just before they are about to leave, they will almost certainly press enough cash into your hand to buy the toy, CD, tape, etc. several times over. They leave happy in the knowledge that they have outdone their brother/sister/child (i.e. your mum or dad) yet again. You then need to arrange an armed guard to accompany you to the shops!

Of course, some relatives are in the habit of pressing a coin into your hand as they arrive. This is because they can't wait to demonstrate how much more generous they are than your parents. In order to draw attention to themselves they make a real pantomime out of slipping you a pound coin and saying in a very loud whisper: "Don't spend it all at once!" They then do a wink so large that it makes them look like they've got some terrible eye disorder. But how do you turn this sad-and-lonely pound coin into a much larger banknote? It isn't easy, but you could try this:

Have a £10 note folded in the palm of your hand. As they walk away smugly, having given you the pound coin, you unfold the £10 note, hold it up in the air for all to see and say very loudly: "Wow! A tenner! Thanks a million!"

Your relative will be astonished that their rather sad little gift of a pound has miraculously turned into a big fat tenner – unless you're a member of the Magic Circle, in which case they'll just think that you're showing off.[1]

"Gosh! Is it?" they'll say.

And now you go in for the kill:

"Oh no!" you say. "THIS IS THE ONE MY MUM GAVE ME EARLIER!"

Said relative will bluster, blush, and (hopefully) dip their hand in their pocket and produce more dosh.

A POINT TO REMEMBER:
You should not really expect relatives to give you money every time they come round. Although, why else would they be there?

Subs

What are they?
Well, one thing they are is those long pointed boats that go underwater, usually after somebody has shouted "Dive! Dive! Dive!". That's what happens in movies, anyway.

But I'm actually thinking of subs as in subscriptions. A subscription is something you have to pay to belong to something. Whether it's the cubs, brownies, the Royal

---

1: In which case, this ploy won't work for you, I'm afraid. Sorry.

Society for the Protection of Birds, or the Mystical Order of the Missing Left Trouser,[1] you'll have to pay a subscription. Incidentally, the Peter Corey Fan Club is free, mainly because it doesn't exist.

Sometimes these subscriptions have to be paid once a year, which isn't so bad. But some of them, like brownies, guides, scouts, etc. are paid every week. This is OK when you're little because your parents are happy to pay your subs for you; this is their way of encouraging you to go.[2] But, as you get older, obviously they are less keen, mainly because there are lots of other things that they have to pay for: school trips, library fines, next door's broken windows, and so on. And so there will come a time when your parent(s) will tentatively suggest:

"Maybe you would like to pay your own scout's subs this week?"

Are they completely *mad*? Surely the words *like* and *pay* are not legally allowed to be in the same sentence, are they? But no, even though your parents probably are, technically speaking, mad (all parents are), in this instance they are totally serious and acting – as far as they are concerned anyway – totally rationally.

1: The Mystical Order of the Missing Left Trouser doesn't exist, so please don't try and join it.
2: You probably wouldn't be seen dead there otherwise!

How to cope

Of course, the simplest way around this is to give up whatever it is that you're being asked to pay the subs for. It's amazing how quickly things lose their charm when they stop being free. But maybe you don't want to give up this particular activity. Maybe it's fun; or maybe it's a great way to meet girls (or boys); in which case it won't be the scouts. In my experience, the scouts was a great way to meet trees, or useful bits of string, but never girls.[1]

I'M TRYING FOR MY "TYING A TREE IN A KNOT" BADGE

Nevertheless there is more to life than the opposite sex, apparently, and it just so happens that you want to stay in this particular club or organization, for whatever reason; but you simply can't afford it. So what do you do?

There is the straightforward approach: you go to the parent in question and say:

"I desperately want to stay in the Colin Chuffney Memorial Trainspotting Club, but I just can't afford to."

This approach is honest, wholesome and to the point. So obviously it's not likely to work, because parents do not understand any of these concepts. Therefore, a bit of subterfuge is needed:[2]

1: Actually I'm lying, but I'm not prepared to go into details!
2: Or SUB-terfuge.

A few minutes before you are due to leave the house to attend the Colin Chuffney Memorial Trainspotting Club (or maybe it's the WigglyBum Free-form Dance Ensemble), you walk into the room, clearly not ready to go.

"Aren't you going this week?" asks concerned parent.

"Nah. I thought I'd give it a miss."

"But I thought you really enjoyed it?"

At this point there are a number of routes the conversation can take. I will outline two of them:

ROUTE A:

"Yes, I do love it – it's the best thing ever. But I just can't afford the subs."

Because you are delivering this bombshell so close to the time that you would normally need to leave the house, the parent does not really have time fully to assess the implications of what you are saying, beyond the fact that you want to go, can't afford it, and are clearly upset. To be honest, anything more complicated than that would probably be beyond their comprehension anyway; they are adults after all. Their most likely response is:

"Let's talk about it later. If I drop you off in the car we might just make it. And don't worry about the subs – I'll take care of those."

Of course, not all parents are this shallow. There are some parents who are frankly so devious that they should be banned by law from being parents in the first place. For this type of parent a more convoluted route is needed.

ROUTE B:

"Do you want the truth?" (A sure cue for a lie!) "I only ever joined [NAME OF CLUB] because you wanted me to. I know that you were champion trainspotter/top dancer/ niftiest ninja when you were my age, and I was trying to be as good as you."

YOUR FATHER WAS THE TOWN'S CHAMPION MILK FLOAT SPOTTER SIX YEARS RUNNING...

OH, DEAR

"So it's not a question of money then?"

At this point don't say:

"Of course not."

After all, it *is* a question of money, and you need to make sure that money stays in the frame. So play the money down but don't blow it out, as in:

"Weeeeellllll… Not entirely."

Guilt will kick in. For the parent, not for you! This is surprising, I admit, but parents are not totally impervious to guilt, even though most other emotions are a complete mystery to them. The result of the guilt will be something along the lines of:

"Yes. You're not bad. Obviously you'll never be quite as good as me because you've got your father's knees/ mother's teeth;[1] but we can't have you giving up. How would it be if *I* paid for you to go?"

"Great! Any chance of a lift as well?"

DON'T PUSH IT!

Thank you letters

What are they?

Letters to relatives, friends of your parents etc., who have sent you gifts at Christmas or birthday. They are

1: They always blame the other parent.

also a *pain*! And what are they all about? After all, when you give somebody something do you expect a letter of thanks? Every time you feed your gerbil do you rush to the postman expecting a badly scrawled thank you note signed with a paw print?

IS THAT A THANK YOU NOTE FROM YOUR GERBIL?

NO. IT'S A COMPLAINT. APPARENTLY IT WANTS BETTER QUALITY FOOD!

Of course you don't! You give, with no thought of reward. But what you have to remember is that adults are different, in case you hadn't noticed. They positively *bathe* in gratitude. Which is why, every time they slip you a 50p piece when nobody's looking, they make sure that the whole world sees them do it. If that doesn't sound as though it makes sense it's because this is adults we're talking about. You'll probably find that they keep your thank you notes in a scrapbook. Actually they don't, of course; some adults don't even read them. It might be an idea to find out which adults read the notes and which don't. That way you'll know whether or not you have to worry about tricky stuff like spelling and so on.

I DON'T SEE WHY I HAVE TO WRITE EVERYONE'S THANK YOU NOTES!

Whether they read them or not, *not* sending a thank you letter can seriously affect your chances of getting anything half decent next time.

How to cope

The most boring thing about thank you letters is thinking of things to say to people that you hardly know/ hardly like/hate with a passion. Close relatives are not so difficult because you probably have more in common with them. This is just as well, because relatives that you see regularly are far more likely to keep hinting about not getting a letter.

Actually, the people who cause most hassle when it comes to thank you letters are parents; and so they are the ones you need to impress. Most parents are not happy to let you write your thank you letters on your computer. They feel that the sincerity of the "thank you" is in some way weakened by it being in type. This is just one of the many mysteries of the adult brain. Frankly, the only way most of your relatives will ever be able to *read* the letter is if it's printed! This is quite a useful argument to use when trying to persuade your parents that the letters would be better written on the PC, but don't overdo it or they may arrange for you to have private handwriting lessons. A much better argument is the one that goes:

"If I do them on the computer then I can scan in pictures of the family, the dog's boil and loads of other interesting stuff."

You might even be able to persuade other members of the family to add their own bits, so that a boring "thank you" letter becomes a really "interesting" family newsletter. This should work extremely well, although you will need a computer, printer, scanner and all the necessary software. Have you got all that? No? Oh well, you'd better get writing then![1]

Tokens
See BOOK TOKENS, GIFT TOKENS

Ugly shoes

Imagine the situation: you've been given some birthday money. You've seen these amazing shoes in the window, that you've been drooling over for weeks. Maybe you've even told your parent(s). And maybe, in a rash moment, they've even said: "Oh well, you'll be able to buy those with your birthday money, when it's your birthday."[2] You go into the shop, having managed to give your parent(s) the slip. Yes! The shoes are still in the window! You tell the assistant what you want, and they say: "I won't be a minute." and disappear into the bowels of the shop. They then return with the most startling array of disgustingly ugly shoes that you've ever seen in your life.

ARE THESE SHOES OR THE BOXES THEY COME IN?

1: Use your thank you letter to tell the various relatives that you are saving up for a computer, scanner, printer, etc. That way it's not a wasted opportunity.
2: Parents say this sort of thing so that you realize that *they* realize that birthdays and birthday money are in some way related. They just don't know *how*.

You tentatively say:

"What about the ones in the window?"

"They're in the window, I'm afraid."

"Yes. Can I have those?"

"No."

"Why not?"

"Because they're in the window."

"Well, can't you get them out?"

"No."

"Why not?"

"Because they've been super-glued in, in case somebody tries to steal them."

"What about if somebody tries to *buy* them?"

"Buy them?"

This is said as though the mere idea that anyone would want to go into a shoe shop and buy shoes is just too bizarre to contemplate.

How to cope

You can't. Sorry. It's just one of those horrible facts of life that, if you go into a shoe shop you will come out with ugly shoes, whether your parent is with you or not.

In fact, you might be better off if you take a parent with you and adopt the scam outlined under "Birthday money". You might, but can you really be seen in public with either of your parents? That could be much, much worse than being seen in public in ugly shoes!

VAT

What is it?

This a special tax that is added to the cost of most things that you buy.[1] VAT actually stands for Value Added Tax, although it doesn't actually add any value to the item, it just makes it more expensive. And that's why you need to know about it. Electrical things, like personal stereos, computer game consoles, and so on, all have VAT added to them. Books, you'll be happy to learn, don't – so if you've bought this book you won't have paid any VAT. If you've borrowed this book from the library you won't have had to pay anything, except a huge library fine when you forget to take it back. And since the fine will almost certainly be more than the original cost of the book, you'd be better off buying the book in the first place. Children's clothes are also VAT free. And this explains your parents' reaction to you growing, because once you get to a certain height you can no longer get into children's clothes, and adult clothes cost much more money.

How to cope

Stay short and read books. Although this won't help you get that computer game that you're so desperate for. Unfortunately, there's really no way round the dreaded

---

1: It's actually 17.5 per cent, or £17.50p for every £100; isn't that interesting!

VAT, so if you do want something that has VAT added, you're going to have to use the skills explained elsewhere in the book, and don't mention the price!

Wages

What are they?

Most jobs result in a salary, or wages. This is a sum of money paid either weekly or monthly in return for you doing a job. Some of you will have paper rounds and so you'll already know roughly, what wages are all about. They should really be called WAGESL, standing for Working 'Ard And Getting Ever So Little because, frankly, wages for the sort of jobs that you are allowed to do are not that good. They also have none of the "perks" that jobs have in the adult world.[1]

Take a paper round, for instance. Do you get more money if it's raining or snowing? Of course not! Does the paper shop provide special clothing so that you are protected against wind, rain, snow, large dogs and rabid hamsters? Of course they don't! But if you were an adult you'd not only have all this supplied with the job, but you'd also get bonuses, sick leave, maternity leave, a pension, a company car, and all sorts of other things that almost make the job worth doing. Almost, but not quite.

However, none of this need worry you if you're under 13, because you're too young legally to have a paper round.[2] But you can still get wages, if you're crafty.

How to cope

I have said elsewhere in the book that you should try and avoid fixed rates for jobs around the house because it's

---

1: Which is the same world that you live in, only a bit taller.
2: Or sweep chimneys, mop sewers or any jobs that you might have been offered!

often very difficult (i.e. impossible) to get the rate improved once it's been set. Remember these rates are set by parents, and parents don't understand things like inflation. Also, I'm thinking in terms of wages not being something you get paid for doing a particular job, but more a sum that you get on top of your pocket money for doing a range of jobs around the house. Don't panic! I'm not thinking about a particularly large range! In fact, I'm thinking of a very small range indeed; probably jobs that you would do anyway, such as cleaning your shoes, tidying your room – no, hang on, I think they're probably bad examples! Look, I'll leave you to work out exactly which jobs you feel fall into this category. After all, you know your parents better than I do, and therefore you probably have a clearer idea of what you can get away with. Now you may be thinking: "Hang on a minute! Why bother with wages? Why not just get an increase in pocket money?" So let's get that out of the way right now. Let us suppose that your pocket money is £5 (we can all dream!) and you negotiate wages of an extra £3 for walking the dog, cleaning up the garden after the dog and doing the washing-up three times a week.

That sounds about right to me. But why don't we just call it £8 pocket money and be done with it? Simple; because when you want to negotiate a pocket money increase your parent(s) will base it on £8, which is quite a decent amount of pocket money, as opposed to £5, which sounds like a lot less. Also the advantage of receiving two separate sums is that you have two sums to renegotiate (i.e. increase) instead of just one. One bit of advice: make sure that you renegotiate your pocket money and your wages separately. I suggest you try for more pocket money about a month after each birthday. Your argument should be that now you're a year older you need more money. On the wages front, listen out for any talk about your mum or dad getting a pay rise themselves; this would definitely be a good time to move in and start talking about inflation and the way that the going rate for dog-walking has gone up. The dog is also older and therefore harder to walk.

If you approach all these negotiations with a reasonable amount of caution, you should be able to increase your income month on month. Add to this any one-off payments you get for cleaning the car or mowing the lawn, and you could soon be earning more than your parents!

"X" amount

What is it?
This is the sort of thing people say when they don't want you to know exactly how much they're talking about. Parents use it so that you won't be able to work out much they earn.

Example: "Soandso said that if I give him "X amount" he'll let me have the whatdyermcallit." Talking in code or what? Let's face it, that could mean anything. It could mean:

"Johnnie Elastic said that if I give him £20,000 in used notes he'll let me have the jag." Or it could mean:

"Mr Protheroe said that if I give him 50p he'll let me have the bag of home-made boiled sweets his wife made."

You can never tell, but it's safe to assume that if parents talk in code they've got something to hide. Either that or they've been watching too many James Bond movies.

You see, their biggest fear is that if you find out how much they earn you'll be pushing them for much more pocket money, wages, birthday and Christmas money, etc. Likewise, they'd never get you to clean the car again, because you'd turn round and say: "Cor! The amount you earn you could buy a new one every time the car got dirty!"

How to cope

There's really nothing to cope with. But it is worth mentioning that if your parents use the term "X amount" they are far more likely to be disguising a *large* sum than a *small* one. If they use the term a lot then this could be a good time to move in, and try and negotiate a "pay" rise.

A word of warning. It's possible that if you push your negotiations too much your parents will say something along the lines of: "You don't pay *us* for being your parents."

This is the kind of ludicrous logic that only a parent is capable of, and is quickly dismissed by saying: "No, but I never wanted you as my parents. I wanted Mr and Mrs Hodges up the road who've got seven cars and their own swimming pool." That'll shut them up!

Your own wheels

What are they?
In your case, we're probably talking about a bike, although no doubt you're already dreaming of the day when you can have your own motor. But for the moment you're going to have to make do with a bike. There are two distinct types of bike: the one you save up for and buy yourself, otherwise known as the Dream Machine, and the one your parents buy you, otherwise known as the Complete Waste of Space.
Why is it that anything your parents buy you is almost certainly going to cause the Fashion Police to turn up on your doorstep, batter your door in with metal bars and cart you off to be tortured and interrogated within an inch of your life? When will parents realize that rubbish

often costs the same as decent stuff?[1] Never, frankly. When it comes to bikes, parents are very fond of saying things like: "What do you need 20 gears for?" What does your mum need 30 pairs of shoes for? After all, she's only got one pair of feet.[2] This demonstrates a total lack of understanding of the way a modern bike works. The more gears you've got the more energy you save when you're cycling. And saving energy is what life in the twenty-first century is all about. This is not an exercise bike we're talking about here; it's an efficient form of transport. Unfortunately, your parents' childhood memory of a bike is something *their* parents bought them. It had three gears and a chain that kept coming off. With some of the bikes I've seen recently it's hard to work out where the chain *is*, let alone how it comes off.

So the obvious choice is buying your own "wheels"; fast, efficient and with low maintenance. The only problem is *how*.

How to cope
Parents respond well to the idea that their children are saving up for something. It almost doesn't matter what, although if they got wind of the fact that you were saving up in order to be able to fill your dad's bath water with piranhas, they might have something to say about it.

So you want a bike; a big flashy one with more gears than is feasible on a bike of that size, and all the latest stuff; exactly the kind of bike that your parents will never let you have in a thousand years. So throughout the saving-up period you've got to work on getting them used to the idea. There are two things to emphasize:

The enormous range of safety features that your chosen bike has, whether it has them or not. And...

1: Unless the rubbish has got designer labels.
2: As far as you know.

The massive effort that you are putting into the whole saving experience.

Both of these will impress your parents enormously, because they both demonstrate how *mature* you're being. This sort of thing impresses parents, mainly because maturity is something that they're not too good at themselves. If you play this exactly right you may even get your parents chipping in the odd few pounds every now and again, just to speed the whole process up. A word of caution: Never, ever show them a picture of your chosen bike unless you want the whole thing to go pear-shaped. Pear-shaped bikes are no use at all.

Eventually you'll have saved enough money to buy your dream machine. You take yourself off to the shop to collect it. DO NOT accept a lift from either (or both) of your parents. You really DO NOT want them in the shop with you whilst you're buying your bike; partly because they'd try to get you to buy a *sensible* (i.e. ugly) one, and partly because, if the shop owner sees your parents, he might assume that you're all escaped lunatics and refuse to serve you.

Having bought your bike, you take it home. Leave it outside and do one last bit of PR about the wonders of the bike, how having so many gears is really a safety feature and so on. Show them the safety helmet, reflective armbands and lights that you've bought to go with your new bike. Then, and only then, let your parents see it. Make sure that while they're looking at it you continue to jabber on about how brilliant it is. This will prevent them having any kind of a conversation about what *they* think about the bike.

None of this will make your parents *like* the bike, but probably the worst thing they'll do is shake their heads and assume that your poor choice of wheels is in some way to do with hormonal imbalance,[1] which is something neither they nor you have any control over. Problem sorted; you have the bike of your choice, and you've also demonstrated that you're capable of being careful with money at the same time.

A word of advice: if you are saving for a bike make sure that you allow enough money for a decent helmet. Yes, I know some of them look a bit nerdy, but there are a few cool ones and if they help save your life what does it matter if you look a bit silly? Reflective bits are also important, because you do want motorists to see you cycling along. But to me the most important things are bright lights, especially if you think you might need to ride your bike at night (most people do). Yes, I know that a lot of cyclists rely on reflectors these days, but unless a car's headlight beam hits the reflector directly they don't show up at all, and even when they do they're pretty pathetic. Lights, on the other hand, not only help

1: Hormonal imbalance can be used to excuse pretty well anything, as long as you don't overdo it.

you be *seen*, but they also help you to *see*; two things that I would have thought were essential when riding a bike at night. Sorry; as you know I don't normally preach at you, but I've seen too many people knocked off their bikes not to mention it. Thank you. Lecture over. Let's go back to being funny (ish!).

Zee end bit

What is it?

Well, it's the end of the book. Sort of. Regular readers of my books will know that I sometimes have to cheat a bit in the A–Z section because I can't always think of things that match the letters of the alphabet. X usually gives me a problem, but this time it's Z. So I've cheated. So what? It's my book and I'll do as I please!

I hope that all of the above stuff has helped you understand the many, many different sides to money; how to get it, how to hang on to it, and what to do with it when you get it. Of course, there are millions of things that I haven't told you. I haven't mentioned, for instance, that Henry VIII added cheap metal to gold and silver coins in Tudor times, presumably to save money.

'ERE! HOW COME THIS GOLD COIN IS TIN COLOURED?

THAT'S RARE, PERHAPS IT'S WORTH SOME MONEY?

When his daughter Elizabeth I came to the throne she had the coins remade putting the gold back in.

I haven't told you that French soldiers serving in Canada in 1685 were paid in playing cards because their wages were often delayed in being shipped from France.

Nor have I mentioned the California gold rush in the mid-nineteenth century; or the fact that after the First World War (1918) inflation ran so high in Germany that by 1923 money was almost worthless; workmen were being paid twice a day, and taking their pay home in huge wicker baskets. A loaf of bread cost hundreds of marks.

In Italy in the 1970s, there weren't enough small coins to go round, so shop keepers used to give bags of sweets as change! In Vietnam, they used lipstick as money, and during the Second World War people sometimes used cigarettes.

I also haven't told you that they mark the edges of coins to stop people forging them; this is called milling. Check a pound coin, you'll see what I mean.

Did I mention that coins were exchanged as love tokens in medieval times? I don't think I did. I could also have told you that audiences in Shakespeare's time used to throw coins at the actors; occasionally they hit one – that soon shut him up!

Did you know that in Fiji they used to use whales' teeth for money? Well, you do now. In fact, there's lots, lots more to discover about money. A book like this can only scratch the surface. But one thing I can tell you is the secret of money. How to make loads and loads of it. Would you like to know that? Would you like to be so rich that you couldn't count your money even if you stayed up all day and night and didn't even have time to watch telly? Well, here it is:

THE SECRET OF MONEY

Oh no! I've run out of book! You'll just have to find out the secret for yourselves. And if you do … do you think you could let *me* know what it is, please?